MY SON SAVED ME

MATTHEW SHORES

This book is designed to provide a firsthand account of one man's COVID journey and is not meant to serve as medical advice.

The work is the particular property of the author. Produced by human intellect and was in no way created or manipulated by an AI (Artificial Intelligence) program.

Cover Design
Anya Kelleye Designs
Anyankelleye.com

Published By
Brackish Publishing
brackishpublishing.com

This book is dedicated in honor of all the doctors and nurses at Lexington Medical Center who brought me back to life.

This book is dedicated in memory of the over seven million people worldwide who have lost their life to this dreaded virus. To the families of those we lost, may God provide you comfort and peace knowing your lives will never be the same.

PROLOGUE

I t was a cold winter morning in the Midlands of South Carolina. My wife, Tracy, and my eleven-year-old son, Warner, had the house to themselves, along with our five-year-old Havanese, Zoe. It was not your typical Christmas morning as my family was concerned over my hospitalization with COVID-19.

The house was excessively decorated, of course, as Christmas decorating is one of my wife's favorite pastimes. Each year, I bring downstairs approximately twenty boxes full of... well, let's just call it stuff! From fake Christmas present boxes to stockings to winter photos that replaced our regular décor.

This was not the best Christmas. My mother-in-law, Janet, who lives with us, was in a separate hospital in the capital city of Columbia. as she had a mild case of COVID, but due to her being over the age of 70, she needed to be hospitalized and monitored as we were in the peak time of this deadly pandemic. Hospitals were stretched to their maximum capacity and thousands of people in the U.S. had already succumbed to this deadly virus.

As Tracy and Warner snuggled in bed together trying to stay warm, questions were running rampant through their minds. Was there going to be a phone call and if so, when? What news would be shared from my excellent care team at Lexington Medical Center? Would the update be news they were dreading?

The team of doctors had been providing daily updates on my status, which at this point was not good. I had been in the hospital for a week and all that time was spent in the ICU, with the past three to four days on a ventilator because my lungs were failing. My lungs were filled with COVID-19, and the doctors had previously told my wife I didn't have a good shot at coming off the ventilator alive. At one point, my wife was told to "prepare for the worst."

They were silently praying in bed at approximately 8:30am when the phone rang. Warner jumped from his seated and very comfortable position, fearing the worst. Tracy hesitantly answered the phone. On the other end was one of the COVID specialized doctors, and Tracy was fearing the worst news possible.

Please don't tell me my husband is gone, she thought as the doctor was beginning to speak. It took my wife a few seconds to process what the doctor was telling her, and then she said softly. "Could you please repeat that again?"

THE POWER OF PRAYER!

PART ONE

CHAPTER 1

CHILDHOOD

I was born in December 1972 to my father, Ronald Lee Shores, and my mother, the late Joan Diane (Logan) Shores, in Washington D.C. My first month of my life I spent in Prince Georges County (or simply known as PG County for those from Maryland). A month into my life, my family, including my older brother by four years, Ronnie, moved to a small town in Western Montgomery County called Poolesville, approximately thirty minutes from DC. Poolesville was just 5=five small miles from the Historic Whites Ferry, which crossed the Potomac River separating Maryland from Northern Virginia. My father moved there so he could be closer to Germantown, a short twenty-minute commute as he worked for the Department of Energy.

My father was born in St. Clairsville, Ohio and my mother was born in a nearby coal mining town of Glencoe. They were high school senior sweethearts. Three years after graduating high school, my mother completed nurses' training at Ohio Valley General Hospital while my father was attending West Liberty University, across the border in West Virginia. They got married on August 20, 1966, and after my father graduated college in 1967. They moved shortly thereafter to Upper Marlboro, Maryland, so my father could work for the Federal Government.

Our family visited Ohio often as my three living grandparents were there. My father's father, Asa, passed away in 1970 before I was even born. My grandfather worked as a caretaker on an estate called Alken Ridge. I have pictures of my father as a young teenager working the tractor, cutting the grass on this massive piece of land. My father's mother, Mary, remarried, and owned a newsstand in the center of St. Clairsville. I remember from the young age of five visiting her newsstand, full of papers, candy, and a pinball machine. Ronnie and my cousin, Sherri, played pinball, while my cousin, Lori and I would help Grandma run the cash register. Now, young people, this wasn't today's version of a cash register. If something was worth twenty-two cents, you pressed down hard on the twenty-cent button until it made the famous "cha-ching" sound and then the two-cent button. You pressed down a lever to open the cash register, where most of it was filled with coins and a few one-dollar bills. I did remember seeing a few five-dollar bills and thinking to myself how rich they were.

Across the street from my grandmother's newsstand was the place that everyone from St. Clairsville knew was the best place to visit for food… Home

Pizza. They sold small squares of pizza with one slice of pepperoni in the middle. I don't remember how much they cost back then but remember loving walking across the street to have a piece or two and drink some pop. Every drink, except alcohol, was pop. It didn't matter if it was 7-Up, Dr. Pepper, Coke or Pepsi. Just like every drink in Texas is referred to as a Coke or in Maryland was a soda… Ohio had pop. Every time we visited Ohio, until recently, we visited Home Pizza and enjoyed the taste that still makes me think of the Buckeye State. Unfortunately, Home Pizza closed down a few years ago, but the memories remain.

My grandmother was diagnosed with ALS, also known as Lou Gehrig's Disease, and passed away in the summer of 1980. I was only 7 ½ years old. I was too young to understand all about death and what it meant, but the memories of my grandmother still linger in my mind. She loved her two boys, my father and my Uncle Kenny, who was a year older than my father. She especially loved her six grandchildren, even the two she never met. After Uncle Kenny died, I learned he had remarried and had two boys, Kenny and Christopher, who currently live in Colorado. I have met Kenny several times but not Christopher. Two great cousins!

My Uncle Kenny passed in 1998, a mere three days after I returned from my school's sophomore trip to Spain. My memories of my uncle were few, but wonderful. He loved to play and bounce me on his knee. He gave the best hugs in the world. After my grandmother's funeral, I never saw him again in person, but his laugh and his smile still linger in my memory.

On my mother's side of the family were my grandparents, Dave Logan and Sarah (Rosepapa) Logan. Grandad Logan was born in Scotland in 1908, and his entire family moved to the United States as soon as World War I ended in 1918. To this day, I can still hear that Scottish accent as clear as day as he played his favorite card game, Euchre.

"Gee-Suss Key-Rist," he would shout across the kitchen table at whomever his partner was, "Why in the hell did you play that?" he would exclaim every time he lost a game.

You would assume he was a very fiery person, but when not playing cards, he was calm and always laughing. He was an awesome grandfather to Ronnie and me. He took us to Wheeling Downs to watch the greyhound races. Every race bet a $1 on the 1-8 combo, but before each race would begin as the dogs would parade down the front of the track, the last one to poop would be his. He would stride to the counter and slam down a dollar and bet on that dog. It seemed that most of the time his attention to detail was right as the last dog to poop would often win. As we would leave the races, he would slip my brother and I a crisp $1 dollar bill and laugh. What a character!

My Grandmother Logan's family, the Rosepapas, were originally from Hungary. My grandmother was the best cook and made almost everything homemade. Her Amish style noodles were extraordinary. Every time I visited, she made me fresh pumpkin pie and would make my brother at least two dozen chocolate chip cookies. There was always pop in the fridge, as Ronnie and I would sit at her table and eat and drink. Other times, we would stand with Grandad at the edge of the "crik" as he called it (known to Americans as a creek) and fish. The memories of Glencoe are so much fun to remember.

My mother had an older sister, Joyce, and a younger brother, Dave. My Aunt Joyce was eight years older than my mother, while my Uncle Dave was eight years younger. Sixteen years separated my aunt and uncle. My Aunt Joyce was also a nurse and had the best cackle and the most soothing, loving voice. She and my Uncle George lived in Dover, Ohio, about an hour and a half from Glencoe along Interstate 77 and only a half hour from Canton, where the Pro Football Hall of Fame is located. About five miles west of Dover was Sugarcreek, the beginning of Amish country. You talk about some good food. The Amish know how to cook some soothing food. The best part about visiting them was getting to eat the cinnamon rolls that she would buy in Sugarcreek… food memories. Notice a trend yet?

My Uncle Dave came to live with us after he graduated from Ohio University, where he played in the marching band. He was dating Linda, who later became my aunt, but I started calling her Aunt Linda long before they married. My Uncle Dave was by far the tallest member of the immediate family, a good 6 foot 4 inches tall. He towered over my five-year-old scrawny body. He would take my mom for a motorcycle ride, and I would scream as the booming sound motorcycles made scared me to death. After a year, he moved to Potomac, about twenty-six minutes away from my hometown. We would visit often and every time I entered their townhome, my first mission was to make five putts on their putting machine, which stretched a good six feet. I loved each time I made a putt because the machine would spit back the ball to my putter, so I didn't have to move.

In late 1980, they moved to San Jose, California, where they reside to this day. They became season ticket holders to San Francisco 49ers games in the old Candlestick Park and had end zone seats and saw "The Catch." This was the infamous game in the 1982 NFC Championship (1981 Season) where the Dallas Cowboys held a late 27-21 lead with one minute in the fourth quarter. Former Notre Dame QB, Joe Montana, on third and goal, rolled right looking for a receiver and as Ed "Too Tall" Jones was bearing down on him, threw up a high pass that was sailing out the end zone until WR Dwight Clark snatched the ball out of the sky, caught the winning touchdown and sent to the Niners to their first Super Bowl, which started a dynasty. Uncle Dave and Aunt Linda's seats were in the opposite end zone, but to this day, remember that game like it was yesterday!

Just a short week after my Grandma Shores died, while we were all still in Ohio, my Grandad Logan died of a sudden heart attack. I remember my dad speeding down the back roads from St. Clairsville to Glencoe as we got a call that an ambulance had been dispatched to try to revive my grandad. As we got to the house, I remember all my family members, including my favorite cousins (known as FC) from Cleveland, Lynn and Lori, all crying and sobbing. Of course, I was only seven and really didn't understand it all. The one vivid memory I have of that day was my mother on the ground sobbing uncontrollably as my father tried to console her. Apparently, when you're a daddy's girl, the death of your father changes you forever. My mom was never the same after that awful day in August 1980. For years, when even mentioning Ohio, she would cry. I never understood how that felt until many years later.

Our childhood memories shape us into who we are today. Whether the smells of fresh pie or recalling unique voices in our heads give us our history. Nothing beat listening to my Grandma Logan talk about God, as I later learned from her, it's all about...

THE POWER OF PRAYER!

Chapter 2

SPORTS

Our family was very sports oriented. I remember watching my brother play soccer, basketball and baseball, which were mostly coached by my dad. We would go together to every sporting event played. To be honest, my brother was more of a "natural" athlete than I was, as every sport came easy to him. I watched him intently to learn the nuances of each sport, so I felt when I entered my time to play, I was a little ahead of the curve than most of my teammates.

In the first grade, I started playing soccer. This game came very easily to me, as I had a knack for scoring goals by being at the right place at the right time! I ended up playing soccer until my senior year in high school. My senior year, I tied for the most goals scored that season but was mostly remembered for my "near-misses" and goalpost hits. I hit at least four cross-bars on shots during my senior year, and our team could have ended with a better record than we did, but we enjoyed our season.

I learned to play baseball starting in the first grade. I was a pretty good hitter for my tiny frame and was accurate in my throws. I played baseball until the eighth grade, when I had to decide between baseball and my true love of tennis. My highlight of youth baseball came in the fifth grade, as our team comprised of fourth and fifth graders played in the championship game against Fox Chapel, comprised mostly of sixth graders. We started the game terribly as our ace pitcher gave up an immediate nine runs without recording an out. My dad, who coached along with Mr. Haddaway, decided to put me in as pitcher. I don't know what got into me that day, but I pitched lights out, and it helped as my left-handed pitching seemed to fool the hitters. I didn't throw with a lot of heat, but the ball moved. With each strikeout earned, I gained more confidence. At the end of the day, our offense clicked and won 13-9 as I pitched a no-hitter for the entire six innings. As we gathered after the game, I was presented with an awesome keepsake... the game ball signed by the coaches and all my teammates. To this day, that ball still resides in my upstairs room for display. There is no greater feeling than winning a championship!

I started playing basketball in the third grade. My dad coached us until the eighth grade, through multiple leagues. Early in my career, I hogged the ball and took most of the shots, which I sometimes made but as the years progressed and my teammates got bigger and bigger and I remained a small little runt, I had to learn to rely on my teammates to get the job done. I played point guard and was a true distributor. When I got to high school, I sat out my ninth grade for the JV team but was still involved as a scorekeeper. Then the impossible happened before my sophomore year... they announced a high school 3-point line. I could finally make a difference with my tiny self, shooting from long range and making the big shots. I played JV for my sophomore and junior seasons. I learned to become more aggressive and assertive during my junior season as my confidence rose.

The highlight of my junior season was in January 1989 against Sherwood. We were down 7 with 30 seconds left when I hit a 3-pointer, stole the inbounds pass and gave it to my teammate who got fouled. After a few made free throws along with timely rebounding from my teammates, we tied the game with 14 seconds left. Sherwood quickly came down the court and missed a jumper and I grabbed the rebound and called for an immediate timeout with three seconds left. Knowing we had to go the length of the floor and with the entire Sherwood team lined up at mid-court and beyond, I asked Joe to inbound the ball to me near their foul line and then heaved up a prayer. From seventy-five feet, the ball seemed to stay in the air for minutes, and as the ball traveled, I knew it had a chance, and then SWISH! Nothing but net! The buzzer sounded and my miraculous long distance heave went in, and we won by three. The next thing I knew, the bench cleared, and I was mobbed by my teammates. We had done the impossible! While there was no video taken of the game, I am sure if it was, it would have made Sports Center Top 10 plays!

My senior year, I played varsity, and our team was loaded, but had been burned the year before by a last second heave against Milford Mill in the Regional Final. The first sixteen games of our senior year were not good, as we sat with a 6-10 record heading into a must win against Episcopal. We needed a spark to get us going… a talented team but not good results. I was a bench player and while up big in the fourth quarter, we got ever closer to 100 points. This was before the shot clock was introduced in MD High School basketball. With under thirty seconds left, we had scored 97 points, but we needed more. We scrambled on defense and eventually stole the ball, and it was passed to me with a 2 on 1 fast break. Now anyone that knows basketball knows that when on a 2 to 1 fast break, you head towards the basket, and if confronted, pass to your teammate for an easy layup… but I knew 99 wasn't going to spark our fans and the team. I headed down the left side, stopped at the 3-point circle and let go… SWISH! Our crowd went crazy, and as I turned around towards the scoreboard, I saw us at 100 for the first time ever! The buzzer sounded and our student section mobbed the court. We went to the locker room and my teammates started the shower and threw me in with my uniform on. At the top of my lungs, I screamed, "Let's Go!" and promptly turned off the shower. I had done my job and now it was my teammates' turn to finish the season strong… and so we did!

We won our last four games, and then swept all

three playoff games, including the Regional Semifinal "revenge" game against Milford Mill and on March 3, 1990, we won the regional championship 62-50 against Watkins Mill. I didn't play a single minute in the Regional Semifinal or Final, but I didn't care! I sparked our team to a regional championship and an eventual trip to Cole Field House for the Final Four. On March 9th, we entered Cole Field House and, as the shortest on the team, proudly led our team out of the tunnel to an ovation from our entire hometown who traveled the forty-five minutes to College Park to watch us play. We had a big lead in the second half but faltered and lost by four. However, we accomplished our childhood goal of playing in Cole Field House. It's every little boy's childhood basketball dream in the state of Maryland. To this date, no Poolesville boys' team has made it that far. However, in 2018, the Poolesville Girl's Varsity Team, under the tutelage of Coach Swick (who coached us in 1990), won the state championship with a perfect record and was eventually ranked as the 4th best girls' team in the entire country.

With all the thrills of winning in other sports, nothing compared to my favorite sport... TENNIS! I started playing tennis at the age of nine, inspired by watching the 1982 Wimbledon final between two left-ies... John McEnroe and Jimmy Conners. I was so intrigued by the sport and quickly became a really good player. At eleven, my parents got me private lessons and after three lessons, my instructor, who had ties to the Bollettieri Tennis Academy in Florida, approached my parents to invite me to join the academy. Dreams of playing professional tennis danced in my head, but one thing kept me from going... I didn't want to leave my family and friends! I was a very tiny kid at that age and very immature. I decided it was best to stay home but still try to excel at the high school level. My high school tennis career began my freshmen year and my first ever match was #1 doubles. My partner and I lost in a tiebreak, and I was so disappointed. From defeat came good news... my coach saw my potential and promoted me to #4 singles for the rest of the year.

My sophomore year, I played #3 singles and had a breakthrough season. The more matches I played, the more I won. In my junior year, I played #2 singles. With my confidence soaring and a huge workout summer before my senior year, I knew this was probably my last shot. I played #1 singles my senior year, and we entered a new era S We were the smallest school in Montgomery County as a 1A School, Damascus was the only 2A School, and the other twenty-one schools were 3A or 4A schools. Years prior, we had played a private school schedule due to our small size, but in my senior year, we played on both private and county schedules.

It was a grueling senior season, but I came in with the mindset to prove I had a shot to play in college. I was relentless on the court, something I didn't show in other sports. Tennis was my passion, as I was able to use my quickness and hard hitting from both sides to a memorable season. At the end of the regular season, I had a 21-5 record. I had beaten several county players within the top 8 and had also ended up the private schedule as the #2 seed within the 8 teams. Despite my successes, I was not getting looks from any colleges for tennis. From a county perspective, despite all my victories, in order to qualify for the 16-player main draw, I had to play a qualifying match, and it happened to fall on the day of my Senior Prom. My girlfriend could not watch the match (for obvious reasons), so I played in front of one fan... MY MOM! I tried to quicken the pace and eventually won in straight sets and hurried home to get ready for my prom.

The following Monday, I played in the main draw of the county tournament and was matched up against the #3 seed and eventual county champion. I tried my best, but he was just too good and lost 6-4, 7-5. Numerous college coaches were in attendance, but when push came to shove, not a single one approached me after the match. I soon realized that my tennis career was done... or so I thought!

At our annual Senior awards a week before graduation, I received a very huge honor. For every high school in the state, a graduating senior, both male and female, was presented with the US Army National Reserve Scholar Athlete Award. This prestigious award signified excellence in the classroom and on the playing field. My friend Greta and I were honored to win and were presented with gold medals, which I still have. I got to wear it during our graduation and was so proud to have my picture taken with former Redskins great PK Mark Moseley, who was our guest speaker.

This treasured picture is also displayed in my upstairs room as I am a huge Redskins fan!

Sports were a huge part of my youth. Sports teaches you teamwork, resiliency and never giving up. Little did I know how sports would enter my adult life as I learned about...

THE POWER OF PRAYER!

CHAPTER 3

UNDERSIZED AND BULLLIED

As I mentioned, I was small and skinny for my age. In elementary school, I was pretty safe until my brother left after my third-grade year as he entered junior high and high school. In fourth grade, I started getting bullied by several classmates as well as other kids. I was called four-eyes, dweeb and nerd. And let me tell you, those constant words hurt. Some would push me down and get physical. On the way home one day, I was approached and pushed down. I had enough, got up, and connected a small punch to his face. Much to my surprise, the kid stepped back and walked away. I learned a very valuable lesson, and that was sometimes you have to step up and defend yourself. Don't get me wrong, I don't condone fighting, but when pushed past your limits, it's okay to stand up for yourself.

When I got to junior high school, things didn't get better. The bullying and downright meanness didn't come from bullies... for two plus years, they came from my so-called friends. Every time I would walk up to the group, they would laugh, call me names and walk away. While teachers were not watching, they would either smack me on the back of my head or pellet me with spitballs. During these two years, I didn't say a word to my parents or my brother. I didn't want to get them involved and call the school because I feared that would make things worse. My seventh and eighth grade years were the worst two years of my life. A message to young kids out there… be nice to others! Treat others as you want to be treated.

As I entered high school, I began to reach out to others in my grade and found new friends. Most of the male friends were athletes, and the females were mostly popular. Since I was also an athlete, we had common ground and gained respect for each other. For the first time, I was starting to feel comfortable. As my confidence grew, my 'bully friends' from the seventh and eighth grades started to talk to me more. Finally, I was accepted. This was a huge step in my development as a person as I gained confidence, which is vital for those in their teenage years. I went from being a geek to a young kid getting accepted.

During the end of my sophomore year, I was only five feet tall and weighed probably eighty pounds… I was tiny! As soon as the year ended, I hit a major growth spurt and during that summer I grew five inches, got contact lenses and started a job working with youth in our town at a summer sports clinic. When I arrived back at school on the first day of my junior year, I got a lot of stares and comments.

"Matt, is that you?"

"Wow, you look great!"

Let's just say that my junior and senior years of high school were awesome, and I made a ton of friends. However, my journey was just getting started! Little did I know that my mom was silently doing something I understood years later, as it's all about...

THE POWER OF PRAYER!

CHAPTER 4

MY JOURNEY (FAITH AND BEYOND)

Until 1980, we attended the local Presbyterian church, and I loved the people there. I was in their preschool and met friends I would have for a long time. Our pastor even taught me how to swim at age five. However, after my dad's mom and my mom's dad passed away in 1980, we suddenly stopped going to church. I was only seven and didn't fully comprehend death and how it affected my parents. So, for the next twelve years or so, we would spend our Sundays watching our beloved Redskins. This became our Sunday tradition! The most passionate fan in our family was my mom... she loved WR Art Monk! Every play, she would yell at the TV, "throw it to my man!" and every time he would make a catch, she would scream. She jokingly said, at least I thought so, that if something ever happened to our dad, she would marry Art Monk, which I thought was the coolest thing in the world.

Until my senior year, we never talked about church

or religion. I just figured watching football was the way to go. That all changed for me when I met and started dating my senior sweetheart, Jennifer. Her family lived a street over, and even though she was two years younger than me, she was very mature for her age. And to be honest, I was a little immature for my age, so we fit perfectly. I spent a lot of time with her family and her parents were awesome as they welcomed me as one of their own. Her little brother and I would play catch together, as he was a talented baseball player at the young age of ten. He was a pitcher, and I tried to be a catcher for him to practice, but dang he just threw the ball too hard!

Jennifer was a fun-loving, family-oriented blonde with captivating eyes. She was on the Pom squad and played basketball and softball. From the moment we met, we truly enjoyed each other's company. We laughed together, and I enjoyed spending time with her and her family. She asked me a few times about going to church with her, and to be honest, I don't know why I said no, but I did. They say you never forget your first true love, and to this day, the memories of my senior year with Jennifer stick with me. She taught me about the importance of family and always respecting your parents. Jennifer, thank you for teaching me some valuable lessons and for being there for me when I needed you.

After high school, I attended St. Mary's College (MD) for three semesters. I was only 17 for my entire first semester, and in retrospect, I should not have gone away to school. Suddenly, there was alcohol, there were girls, and there was no one forcing you to go to class. So, what did I do... nothing! I took a perfect opportunity at a public honors college and blew it! After three semesters, I had earned a 1.5 GPA and failed out. I had to come home to the wrath of two very upset parents. I remember my father sitting me down and telling me I needed to learn responsibility and was going to enlist in the Army, to which I defiantly said no. He then proceeded to tell me that I was going to pay for my own education at Montgomery College while working at the same time. It was tough love and eventually, I learned my lesson.

During my time at St. Mary's, I was in a long-distance relationship with my best friend's cousin, who happened to live in Columbia, SC. Lesson learned... never date a relative of your childhood friend and neighbor. Because I was so into my girlfriend, I ruined several friendships with those who were special to me. I am not going to mention any names, but the three of you know who you are. Lesson learned... never ruin good friendships over a partner!

Before I started in January 1992 attending Montgomery College in Germantown, an event happened that changed the course of my life. My lifelong friend Bobbi had just lost her dad. She asked me to go to church with her, and because she was a special friend, I said yes. We attended the Sunday service at Memorial United Methodist Church on a chilly January morning. I was instantly drawn to the pastor, Reverend McDonald. He had grown up in Texas and had the traditional booming voice of a typical Southern Baptist preacher, but also had the knack of lowering his voice at just the right moments. I was so intrigued by his sermon. I remember telling Bobbi afterwards that I was definitely going back. For some reason I don't remember, Bobbi didn't go with me again. However, I started to feel like I was part of something bigger than me. Bobbi, thanks for nudging me to attend church again… you changed the course of my future, and I am forever indebted to you for that.

When I attended the next week's service, I met many people who welcomed me back with open arms. I was asked by a member named Rick if I was interested in playing for their church coed softball league. It was a little unique as all women and those men over 55 could hit from their strong side, while males under 55 had to hit opposite handed. I had never tried to hit right-handed, but I learned quickly. For the next four springs and summers, I participated in the league and met some people who I will never ever forget. I figured out later that God was using my love for sports to get me involved in church because he needed to reach me somehow.

Now, back to Montgomery College and a person who influenced my life. My first day on campus, I felt so bad. I had just failed out of a great college and my long-distance relationship had ended. I was in a dark place. But in the place of darkness, came a ray of sunshine… her name is Melinda. I sat down in the back row of Dr. Borkman's government class, looked to my right and saw this smiling face as she introduced herself to me. She asked who I was looking to vote for, and when I said Clinton, her face lit up and proceeded to give me a high five. At that moment, I looked forward to the next time I would see her in class.

We became instant friends. We both liked sports and especially looked forward to the upcoming Winter Olympics. We laughed a lot as we just meshed! For the next two years, we were inseparable. Wherever she went, I went with her. Wherever I went, she went with me. We were often asked if we were dating, but our response was always the same and sometimes in stereo… "We are just friends!"

One of our favorite things was to go ice skating together. There was a rink in Rockville called Cabin John Ice Rink, where we went at least once a month. Afterwards, a stop for ice cream at Friendly's was always in order. We would go to movies, the driving range together. I even tried to teach her tennis, but she kept hitting the ball out of the entire court over the fence and would just giggle hysterically, claiming she just hit a home run.

"Wrong sport, Melinda." I would tell her!

One of my favorite memories of Melinda was driving through the county and stopping at lights. She would roll down her window to get the next car's attention.

When they rolled down their window, she would say, "Pardon me, but do you have any Grey Poupon?"

We would then giggle for at least fifteen minutes. She was such a fun person!

From this friendship, I got to meet Morgan, a little girl who Melinda babysat. You talk about a cute little kid. She had the sweetest voice, and even her mom would let me go with Melinda to take Morgan places. We took her to Disney on Ice, and the Metro in downtown DC for a rally. She had to bring back this very long stick/tree branch that was taller than her. For a time, the three of us seemed like a small family. Melinda and I indoctrinated Morgan with Clinton-Gore talk, and we even went to the inauguration in January 1993. I still have the picture of Morgan on my shoulders, wearing a Clinton hat, with Melinda beside us.

Afterwards, the three of us and Melinda's mom went to McDonalds, where Morgan accidentally pulled down the red fire alarm! She instantly started crying because she thought she was going to jail! We tried to assure her that was not the case, and even the fire chief who arrived shortly after told her the same, but that event might have scared for life! Morgan is all grown up now and is a sports junkie, so it seems Melinda and I did something right by helping to raise her!

I invited Melinda several times to come to church with me, which she did and really enjoyed Reverend McDonald and the people there. She even joined the softball team. During this time, she got to meet and hang out with two of my childhood friends... Steven and Leigh-Anne, whose families went to the same church. Melinda would play third base; I played shortstop and Steven played second base, while Leigh-Anne would keep the score book. Steven was a year behind me in school, and we played youth baseball together for many years. Boy, could he hit the ball a long way!

For years, and many summers, the four of us hung out a lot. While the four of us were hanging out in my parents' basement, watching the 1994 NBA Finals, we saw a moment that most people remember. It's one of those moments in history where you remember where you were... when OJ Simpson made his friend drive the White Ford Bronco while yielding a gun, followed by dozens of police vehicles. We were in just utter shock as we watched the series of events unfold in front of us. We were speechless, which never happened when the four of us hung out together.

Steven now lives in NC and Leigh-Anne lives in VA. To the both of you, I thank you for the friendship and the bond that we got to share, two important friends in my physical and spiritual development!

To this day, more than thirty-two years later, Melinda and I are still very close friends, even with her move to the West Coast and now back to the East Coast. I never took her for granted as I learned my lesson from failed friendships while at St Mary's. We talk often and still laugh on the phone, while occasionally bringing in serious topics to talk about. Melinda, I want to thank you for being that ray of bright sunshine in that time of my life where darkness ensued. You have always been there for me, and I value our friendship dearly. You are loved, my friend! Don't you ever forget that!

During my two-year stint at Montgomery College, I excelled in the classroom. I was inducted into Phi Beta Kappa, the National Honor Society of Junior College. I knew I had it in me to attend a four-year school to complete my bachelor's degree, but where to go? During this time, I had another great friend named Amy who lived in SC. We talked all the time and were very close. As the hot summer approached, Amy suggested I look into schools in South Carolina. In our college library, I found a book called *Barron's Best College Buys in America* and found the school of my dreams... Coker College, now Coker University!

Coker is a private, liberal-arts school located in Hartsville, SC. There were three things that drew me to find out more about Coker. The teacher education program was outstanding, regarded as one of the best in the state. My dream was to be a high school history teacher while pursuing my coaching career in both basketball and tennis. Another plus for Coker was that I could continue playing tennis and receive scholarship money. The final reason I instantly believed Coker was the place for me was the Round Table approach to learning. All classes were taught around round tables, thereby engaging discussion rather than having a professor stand at a lectern and speak for an hour.

I visited my friend Amy in July 1993, and we toured Coker College on July Fourth weekend. I was very fortunate to have the admissions counselor meet us that day to show us around the scenic campus. I spent about an hour on campus, touring the athletic facilities, dorms, and classrooms. I knew right then and there I would eventually enroll in Coker. If it wasn't for Amy, I never would have thought about coming to South Carolina to attend college. I am forever indebted to you, Amy, for showing me how great this state is.

In January 1994, my parents followed me down from snowy Maryland to a warm and balmy South Carolina. The long car ride was filled with anticipation as I embarked on a new journey. Later that day, we arrived in town and began to unload my belongings into my dorm room in Grannis Hall. I was one of the first to arrive that semester, since returning students wouldn't arrive for a day or two. I was warmly greeted onto campus, as most would say to me, "You must be the tennis player from Maryland!"

I soon became friends with a lot of those on campus as back then, Coker was a fun school, but I had also learned my lesson to buckle down and focus on academics. I had to sit out that first year since I transferred without my associate's degree from Montgomery College. In the 90s, the transfer portal didn't exist and transfers had to sit out a year of sports per NCAA rule.

During my first week, I met four ladies who became my lifelong friends... Pamela, Karol, Sharon and Barb. I met them while attending the sophomore class meeting and they were excited about my intentions of being involved in campus activities. During this meeting, I had a chance to meet a man who totally exemplified what Coker was all about... Dr. Jim Daniels, President of Coker College. He approached me, firmly shook my hand, and asked my name and where I was from. After telling him I was from Maryland, he joked that his school, UNC, was going to beat my Terrapins in just two weeks. After the meeting ended, I didn't expect what would happen three weeks later. I was walking across campus headed to my Art Appreciation class when I noticed Dr. Daniels walking towards me.

"Matthew!" he shouted, "congrats to your Terrapins on beating my Tarheels." He shook my hand firmly again as he spoke. "How are you liking it here so far? Are you homesick yet?"

I was shocked the President remembered me and was taking time to get to know me. This concept of a college president engaging with students on such a personal level was unheard of at most schools, but not for this great man! He embodied Coker and the family atmosphere that existed on campus. I began to realize I belonged there and had no intention of ever leaving... I was home!

My first semester quickly passed. I returned to Maryland for the summer and hung out with Melinda while working my new summer job at Energy Federal Credit Union. I got to work with money and meet a ton of great people. However, the three months flew by, and before I knew it, I was back at Coker for the fall semester. The next two years changed who I would become, and I met someone who later became my college sweetheart... Rachel! Her contagious laugh, beautiful eyes and fun-loving attitude had me hooked. Probably the most important thing about her was her faith. She was also a Methodist! We attended Wesley UMC right outside the gates of campus. When we were at her parents' house in Columbia, we attended her home church. There I got to meet her awesome parents, sister and brother, who all treated me like family. I felt like a member of the family rather than a visitor in their home. Throughout the next two years, whenever visiting her family, I felt like I was home. Mind you, that not all parents recognized their daughter's boyfriend as one of them, but her parents sure did. Rachel's dad was also a history major and a veteran, so he shared many stories about his days in the military or stories about his favorite history subjects. We got along so well and I looked up to him as another father figure. Rachel's mom had one of the best laughs I have ever heard.

"We need to fatten you up, Matt," she would say as we prepared dinner. "You are way too skinny!"

Amy's mom would tell me the same thing. And between the two, they tried to fatten me up, but it didn't work too well! It was great to have surrogate moms in SC who looked after me.

During that fall semester, I became very involved in campus activities, joining CCU (Coker College Union), the student programming board as I headed up the intramural program. As the year wore on, I became further involved in campus activities and my self-confidence and self-worth began to grow and flourish. The encouragement I received from Rachel helped me grow as a student leader. As each day passed, I felt like an important part of the college. As the spring semester started, I was ready for one thing... the tennis season. What had been a strong team the year before quickly faded as several key players left Coker. Instead of being a #6 singles player, I played the season as the #3 singles player. Our schedule and the competition in our conference was fierce. I came close to winning several matches that year, but for some reason, like my freshman season in high school, I had to learn to win all over again. It took all season, but my final match I won in a 3-set thriller. To my surprise, a teammate and I were honored as Conference Players of the Week. I knew one thing for sure: I was going to work my butt off to make my senior year a memorable one.

In the fall of 1995, my last year at Coker began. I was appointed as Vice President of CCU, part of the SGA Senate and a member of the Student-Alumni Association, responsible for the Milestone yearbook. We had four key freshmen recruits join the tennis team and enjoyed a successful fall season, finishing at 2-2. I played #5 singles and #2 doubles with Brad, and we formed an instant bond. Our team was tight, and we had a lot of fun times. During our spring season, I was suffering badly from shin splints, but that didn't keep me from playing some of my best tennis. It was my last year, and I made the best of it. I finished with a winning singles record and ended up earned the Team MVP Award. During our conference tournament, I won my last four matches (two in singles and two in doubles) and went out in style during our doubles match by serving aces on my last two collegiate points. Brad made it even more special by jumping over the net, grabbing the ball I last served, giving it to me and thanking me for teaching him the ropes. Brad tragically passed away a few years ago, but I will never forget his friendship and our joy of playing doubles together.

As tennis season ended, graduation was just a few short weeks away. I decided to graduate as my scholarship money was running out for athletics and academics. I needed another two years to complete my teaching certification, but didn't have the money to do so. What was I going to do with just a history degree? Go back home to Maryland and work around the DC area or possibly stay in South Carolina where I felt like I belonged?

In my campus mailbox, I got a notice from the Advancement Office looking for a Development Associate in their department for a full-time job. I quickly put together my cover letter and resume and sent them off to HR. I waited a week or two, but no news. Coker had a special tradition in place called the midnight breakfast, right before the week of final exams, where faculty and staff cooked a late-night breakfast for the students. While eating that night, I saw the VP of Advancement, Frank, and asked him if he had gotten my resume.

"Matt, are you interested in the position? Go get me you resume!"

I raced up the stairs to my dorm room, grabbed my resume, and brought it back down to the dining hall and handed it to Frank.

"I am going to get you an interview before you head back home," he assured me.

The next day, I got a call saying my interview was set for Friday, the day before graduation. While all of my classmates took buses to Myrtle Beach on Thursday, I spent that day in my dorm room packing and preparing for an interview at the same time! What if I got a job at Coker? The prospect of working there excited me, and that night I barely got a lick of sleep.

Friday morning arrived, and I trekked across campus for my 9am interview, not knowing it would last three hours. I got to meet with about fifteen people, including the Athletic Director, Alumni Affairs, and members of the marketing and development teams. I even got to spend time with Dr. Daniels. After my interview, I confidently walked across campus, knowing I had just killed it. However, it was out of my hands, so I prepared to walk across the stage the next morning to receive my degree.

After a very hot graduation in the May sun, my parents and I headed back to Maryland. Not knowing what was going to happen with my possible job prospect at Coker. My father wanted me to get a real job in the DC area. I stalled, knowing I was going to get the Development job, but almost a month had passed and no word yet. Then, on a Wednesday morning, while working at the Germantown branch of Energy Federal Credit Union, I got a phone call from my mom to call Coker. I excitedly dialed the number, hoping for good news, and when Frank answered, he asked if I wanted the job?

I screamed at the top of my lungs, "Yes!" Then we talked about a start date right after July 4th. I was going back to South Carolina to start my career and was on cloud nine for the rest of the week.

A day after spending July 4th on the mall in DC with Melinda and friends, my dad drove a friend's van with a U-Haul attached while I drove my Camry down to Hartsville. Once we arrived in the early afternoon, we spent the rest of the day unpacking and setting up the hand-me-down furniture in my small rental home. My rental wasn't in the best of condition, but it would do until I found something better. Two days later, I started my new job at Coker and hit the ground running. I was so excited to begin my tasks as the phonathon leader, working with Athletic Fundraising, young alumni giving, parent giving and senior gift programs. My first year, we had a great team with Frank, Danny, Pat, James, David, Edie, and the rest of the team. However, there was one special person who got me involved in a way that would later change my life.

Trish was the Alumni Director, and I had worked with her my senior year as treasurer of the Student-Alumni Association. During my first month, she asked me if I had any interest in playing the handbells in her local church, St. Luke United Methodist Church. With my musical background in playing piano for three years, I, of course, jumped at the opportunity.

The following Wednesday night, I went with Trish to St. Luke UMC and met all the ladies in the handbell choir. I was greeted warmly by Shelly, who also served as the youth minister. For the next year, I went to handbells every Wednesday, and we performed several times during the Sunday church service. During this time, I became a proud member of the church and got involved with the youth group. Knowing I would probably stay in South Carolina for a while, my dad assisted me in purchasing my very first home in January 1997.

It was a great starter home on Oak Avenue, just a little less than 1,400 square feet, with three bedrooms, two bathrooms and a fenced in back yard. In February, my parents brought down some used furniture and other household items they had after their move years before. I couldn't believe it; I owned my own home less than a year after graduation.

The first year of work was very successful. The highlight was our team winning Alumni Challenge III, a competition between the twenty-one private college and universities in the state to see who got the highest alumni participation and who would donate at least $10 during the 96-97 fiscal year.

Our theme was "Ring the Bell for Coker". There's been a Bell Tower on campus since 1914 that was rung when winning sports teams would arrive home from away games. Years prior, when Coker was an all-female school, it was rung to wake up for the day, signal for meals and classes. Every Coker alum knew their tradition with the Bell Tower and still today it is a proud symbol on campus.

It was Dr. Daniels dream to get to 50% alumni participation in a given fiscal year before he retired. My job was to make sure that happened and to push us to win the Alumni Challenge III. When June 30th came, we knew we were right at that threshold. After a two-week vacation in early July, I arrived back to good news, which we kept quiet for the next two months... we had reached 52% alumni participation, which was an increase of 25% over the previous year of 27%. I was proud to say I was part of a great team that checked the last box off of Dr. Daniels bucket list as a college president.

When I got back to campus in mid-July, I met a new member of the Coker staff named Kari. She was a beautiful, tall blonde from Roanoke, VA. The moment I met her, I knew I had to get to know her. I was only twenty-four, and she was about to turn thirty, but the age difference didn't bother me. She and I were staff members on a young alumni trip to the North Carolina mountains for a whitewater rafting adventure. We both stayed with Hoyt and Jen in one cabin, and we both slept on separate couches. During the first night, I pulled out the Promise Keepers book from my bag and she asked me why I had that book. I told her I was a Christian and had been given the book by Danny (my mentor) when I had my appendix taken out in an emergency surgery that past May. She began to open up about her faith, and we sparked an instant connection.

After arriving back in Hartsville, tired from a great young alumni rafting trip, we continued to talk in the office the next week. I had mentioned I played tennis, and she told me she also loved to play. That night we went to the Coker tennis courts and played for about an hour and just laughed and had the best time. I have to admit, as the next month followed, we began to connect on so many levels, and we even began to talk about a possible relationship. She had qualities I was looking for in a potential partner, but after learning she was recently divorced, we decided to take things very slow. Then, my life changed forever.

It was Saturday night, August 30, 1997. It was close to midnight, and I was up late as I was such the night owl back in the day. I had been watching Sports Center (shocker!) when I learned that Princess Diana had just been tragically killed during the early morning hours of August 31st in France in a car chase with paparazzi. My phone rang, and it was Kari asking if she could stop by for a few minutes. When she arrived, we sat on the couch, both stunned by Diana's passing. Kari then asked me about my salvation.

"I am going to heaven as I was baptized as a baby." I said.

"Matt, in order to go to heaven, you must accept Jesus as your Lord and Savoir freely into your heart. Matt, do you want Jesus in your life and accept him as your Savior?" No one in my five plus years of church had ever asked me that direct question. I started to question if I was really a Christian and my true salvation. I nodded yes as tears started rolling down my cheek. I felt these warm hands take mine, and she said, "Matt, it's time! Let's pray!" We both closed our eyes; she started a special prayer that I repeated as I finally accepted Jesus into my heart. I started to feel this tingling and warm sensation in my heart that I had never felt before. When we finished praying, Kari wiped the tears from my face, gave me a kiss on my forehead and said, "Matt, your salvation has been determined! You are going to heaven."

We talked for another two hours, just sharing stories about our separate lives and how cool it was that God had brought us together for this special moment. She began to get tired, and I told her to stay on the couch, so she didn't have to drive home. I slowly walked into my bedroom, shut the door and got down on both knees, and began to pray. "Thank you for bringing Kari into my life. I can't thank you enough."

I woke up a few hours later and saw that Kari had left me a note to enjoy church and to be sure to tell my pastor about my life-altering decision. I felt a peace I had never felt before, and I knew it was all because of God. Thoughts of furthering my relationship with Kari raced through my mind, not knowing what God had in store for me at church. I arrived at St. Luke at my normal time of 10:50am and entered the sanctuary in a different mindset. I sat in my normal pew, next to the last pew on the right side. I closed my eyes to reflect on the past twelve hours when I felt a tap on my left shoulder. I opened my eyes, turned around, and was greeted by a beautiful voice.

"Hi, my name is Tracy! I just moved here from Texas." I shook her hand and smiled back at the most beautiful smile and captivating eyes I had ever seen.

Over the course of the next few months, Kari and I continued in our relationship, and I thought I had finally found the one. Unknown to me, Kari had doubts about being in a serious relationship due to the fact that she was thirty and had already married and divorced. I, on the other hand, was getting ready to settle down. As the end of the calendar year drew closer, Kari started to pull away, and over Christmas break, she broke things off. I was devastated! What had

I done wrong? What big mistake had I made. Little did I know what treasure God had in store for me.

In January 1998, I arrived at church and saw Tracy outside the sanctuary. She greeted me and asked if we could sit together. Of course, I obliged and sat on the left side of the church in the fifth row. It was at this moment I knew I had a friend I could count on and be with in church. The next five months followed, and our friendship grew stronger and stronger as we sat together every Sunday, praising God through worship and the singing of hymns.

In late May, I attended the end of year Jaycee convention in Greenville, SC. I was competing in a resume/interview competition as I had won the third quarter contest. The winner of this year-end competition would go on to Las Vegas and represent the entire South Carolina Jaycees at nationals. As usual, I killed my interview, but the decision what not up to me.

That night, we attended a toga party (and yes, I wore a shirt and shorts under my toga). Our Hartsville group was one of the first to arrive. I had one sip of beer and decided to do the famous scissor kick that most of the bass guitar players of rock bands in the 80s always did at concerts. I soon realized why seasoned professionals only did this little stunt. As I came down, my left foot slipped and went out straight in front of me and I felt something tear in my knee. I immediately hit the ground, writhing in pain. I was overcome with nausea and utter disbelief. What had I just done to myself?

After spending almost the entire night in the ER, I

was put in a knee immobilizer and given crutches and told to keep weight off my leg until I could get home to see an orthopedist and get an MRI. A week later, my MRI results came back with devastating news... I had ruptured my ACL. Not torn, it completely ruptured! What in the heck was I going to do? I had massive summer plans, including a trip to CA to see Melinda and flying up to San Jose to see my brother, uncle, and aunt. I even had a tee time booked at the famed Pebble Beach Golf Links. My orthopedist suggested that instead of having surgery, I could strengthen up my quads and hamstrings and, with some rehab, I could wear a brace on my left knee and continue playing USTA Tennis. When I thought all was lost, someone changed the way I looked at life.

I arrived at church the next week and saw Tracy, who obviously was concerned. I told her the story and what my prognosis was.

"Don't worry, Matthew, I will take you to the YMCA after work so I can walk on the treadmill and you can work with weights."

For the next two months, we went to the Y and while I would perform squats, each time I looked up and Tracy would smile and wave at me. She was such a big encouragement and kept me thinking positively. I knew I had a great friend in her.

During the rest of the summer, Tracy and I worked with the church youth group.

Several of the youth, most notably, Kimberly and Fran, would ask us every Sunday night, "Hey, when are you two going to start dating?"

We both emphasized that we were just friends and left it at that. But as time wore on, my feelings started to change. Did I have everything I was looking for right in front of me? One thing was for sure, I didn't want to risk a great friendship and be hurt again.

During that summer, I got to meet Tracy's mom and most of the family she had living in Hartsville. They welcomed me with open arms, and I even got to spend some time soaking my bad knee in her uncle's hot tub, which was great therapy. I remember vividly one Sunday night while soaking my knee, we started talking about football.

"Oh yes, I am a rabid Cowboys fan!" she proudly proclaimed.

For about three to four seconds, a little bit of anger came over me as I remember telling my parents at a young age, "God forbid if I ever marry a Cowboys fan!" God was preparing to test me on that statement.

It was Labor Day weekend, and we spent time with her cousin, his wife and one-year-old son. We made the trek to Myrtle Beach, and I flirted with Tracy the entire time in the back seat with her little cousin between us just giggling. After spending the day in the sand, we went to enjoy a seafood dinner. I loved raw oysters, and Tracy, stating that she would try anything once, tried to down one. Suddenly, she ran toward the bathroom, thoroughly disgusted by what she had just swallowed. I gave her credit for trying, but was assured that would be the last time she would do that.

As we exited the restaurant, her cousin, Carla, approached me and asked if I liked Tracy.

"Of course I do. I think she is awesome," I said.

"Just a hint, but you might want to take action before someone else does," Carla said and left it at that. I was relatively quiet during the two-hour car ride home back to Hartsville. What was I going to do? Do I take a chance and perhaps get rejected??

Once back in Hartsville, I invited Tracy over to my house to have a quick conversation. We sat on my couch, and I spilled my heart to her. I told her I liked her a lot and wanted to have a real relationship built on trust as we both had been burned and cheated on in previous relationships. wanted to take it slow and have a relationship focused around God. I must have spoken for about fifteen minutes and when I finished, I looked into her gazing eyes one last time to get her reaction. She immediately hugged me, and we didn't let go for a while. She thanked me and told me she liked me a lot too and wanted to try dating.

The next three months went by in a flash. In October, while at her house with Shelly watching U.S. Marshals, I started to contemplate our relationship. Was I falling in love? Was she the one I was looking for? The next thing I knew, the movie was over, and I couldn't remember a single scene. I came to a big conclusion that night... I was in love with Tracy and couldn't wait to tell her.

That Thanksgiving, I took her with me to Maryland to meet my parents. I wanted to get their feedback on whether I should take the next step by proposing to her. As we pulled into Poolesville, Tracy got extremely nervous.

"Matthew, I can't do this. Please let's go back to South Carolina. What if your parents don't like me?"

I calmly assured her and made her focus on her breathing. After a few minutes, we left the McDonald's parking lot and soon after, we arrived at my parents' house. My mom and dad were so excited to meet Tracy, and they hit it off immediately. What an awesome three days we spent in Poolesville. I even took her to DC on Friday to show her some of the sights. While Tracy wasn't around, I asked my parents what they thought of her, and my mom gave her the seal of approval. This was the clincher!

Once back in South Carolina, on December 5th, we were going to attend a friend's wedding. The Christmas spirit was in the air. We had looked at engagement rings the night before and one fit right out of the case and Tracy fell in love with her ring. When we got back from Florence, I called the jewelers and had them take the ring off the shelf as I was going back the next morning to purchase. Before our friend's wedding, she asked if we could go back and see the ring one more time, but I told her that the ring was no longer there. You would have thought I had just killed her best friend. Tracy became very sad and depressed that her ring was gone.

We arrived back at my house that Saturday night and she was still depressed over the ring. I couldn't stand it any longer.

"Tracy, what if I told you I had the ring in the house right now?"

She replied, "I would tell you to go get it!"

I went into the bedroom, opened my drawer, pulled the ring out, and put it in my pocket. As I approached the couch, I got down on one knee and pulled out the ring.

"Oh my gosh, it's my ring!" she shouted. I tried to get my words out and make a sweet proposal, to which she replied again, "Oh my gosh, it's my ring!"

"Tracy, will you marry me?" I asked.

To which I got an enthusiastic, "Yes, yes!"

I placed the ring on her finger at 10:02pm. We were engaged, and we couldn't wait to tell the world!

The next six months went by so quickly. On June 26, 1999, in front of our friends and family and, most importantly, with the youth group as our choir, we got married. The best day of my life! My dad was my best man, with my brother and my friend Richard as my groomsmen. Our wedding wasn't until 7:30 pm, so to calm me down, Richard brought in a putter from his golf bag and had me practice putting right-handed or about an hour. This kept my mind off the wedding. I didn't think I was nervous, but Richard knew otherwise.

Tracy is a beautiful woman, but on that day, she was beyond beautiful. She was absolutely breathtaking. I was standing at the front of the church, waiting for her to enter. The doors opened, she saw me, I saw her and smiled, and she proceeded to walk briskly down the aisle. What should have been a slow walk turned into a brisk stroll. I was happy to see her, and she was happy to see me. We turned together towards the youth group as they sang several songs. As I glanced at all the youth, all were smiling as they were singing. These kids were so special to us and to this day, we still keep in touch with most of them, but of course they are all adults and have kids now, which is a weird feeling.

Fast forward to 2003. My job at Coker had previously been put into a part-time position, and Frank did not renew my contract. Tracy's career at GIS was taking off, so we decided to move from Hartsville to Columbia. The hardest part was leaving our best friends, Chris and Amy Thomas. They had a baby named Abby, and this little one was so special to me. I held her all the time, dreaming about what it would be like to have one of my own. We both knew God had a plan for us, but Tracy and I had to be patient. However, our faith was about to be tested.

A year later, on April 27, 2004, I had just gotten home from my job at First Citizens. My phone rang, and it was my dad.

"Matt, your mom is in the hospital and is not well. They are working on her right now!"

I immediately called Tracy, and when I didn't get her, I called my friend, Amy, who made a beeline for my house. About ten minutes later, Amy arrived and as she entered, the phone rang again. It was my dad. My heart went straight into my stomach.

"Matt, I am so sorry, but your mom just passed away."

I fell to the floor and started to cry. Now I knew how my mom felt when her dad passed. I was feeling the same pain and horror. I would no longer see my mom again on this earth. Her dreams of becoming a grandmother had been shattered. My heart was broken.

For many years after my mom's passing, we tried to get pregnant, but to no avail. Tracy was rapidly approaching forty, and we knew time was running out. Finally, in April 2009, Tracy took a pregnancy test, and we were both shocked to see the results... she was pregnant! We immediately thought we were going to have a girl, so we discussed girl's names. She hated my names, and I thoroughly disliked her names. We argued for about three months and could not come to a consensus. Little did we know what we were eventually going to have.

About four months into the pregnancy, we went in for an urgent sonogram. The nurse asked us if we wanted to know what we were having, to which Tracy replied with a girl.

"Mrs. Shores, you are going to have a boy!"

"Are you sure?" Tracy replied. The nurse showed Tracy the real-time image and pointed towards his 'package.' We were both in utter shock. "I don't know what to do with a boy!" she exclaimed.

After leaving the office, we went to Cracker Barrel (a southern staple!) with her mom. We sat puzzled for a few minutes, and then Tracy got the biggest smile on her face.

"Matt, who is my favorite football player?"

"Kurt Warner," I replied. "So, what's your point?"

"Warner! What a perfect name for our son! A man who never gave up on his dreams to become an NFL quarterback. What a godly example for our son to have as his namesake."

"Tracy, I love it!" God knew we needed a boy to agree on a name, and it only took us fifteen minutes... record time!

Fast forward to the early morning hour of 2 am on Thursday, December 10th. I was in the bonus room asleep on the couch with my beloved dog Lilly, who I had gotten as a rescue before Tracy and I became friends. Lilly had a brain tumor, but with the help of medicine, she was able to make it a year without any seizures. She was my baby!

"Matt, wake up! I think my water may have broken," Tracy said.

"What do you mean, you think? Either it did or it didn't."

I got up, grabbed our overnight bags and proceeded with my very pregnant wife to Richland hospital. We arrived at the labor and delivery area and the nurse called in her doctor to determine what was going on.

After a short examination at 6am, the doctor told us, "You are going to have a baby today!"

Tracy called her mom, who quickly came from Darlington. I called my dad in Maryland, but he couldn't make it in time, so he told us to keep him posted. Tracy was frantic, as we had nothing ready for our baby. Her baby shower from work wasn't until the next day. We didn't have a car seat, clothes, nothing! The baby was coming at least four weeks early, but we had no choice!

About 2pm, Tracy started to have major pain. "I

want the epidural NOW!" she shouted to the nurses and me. "Give me the good stuff!" The nurses escorted me out of the room, where I call my friend Richard, all nervous and scared. He calmed me down and told me to soak in the moment and that my life was about to change forever.

"You are ready for this, Matt!"

I came back in and finally Tracy was relaxing. Thank gosh, the epidural was working! To keep my mind in a good place, there was a TV in the delivery room, so I turned on ESPN (shocker!) and kept calm, while standing by Tracy's head keeping her calm. Finally, at 7pm, five nurses and the doctor entered and told Tracy to start pushing. It was time to have our baby!

At 7:58pm, our lives changed forever as our precious baby boy was born. The second he popped out and started crying, I felt something I had never felt before, as my heart tingled just like August 1997 and June 1999... this is what true love really is! Janet, Tracey's mother, took the honor of cutting the cord. Then they laid Warner on the table and cleaned him up.

"Hey Warner, it's Daddy!"

The next thing I knew, the crying stopped as he turned his head towards me. The love continued to pour into my heart. He didn't take his eyes off me. Then, while the doctor was attending to Tracy, the nurse brought me my son, and I held him for the first time. The unconditional love that was staring right into my eyes made me feel like the King of England! This was the best birthday present ever!

I followed two of the nurses while we went to get him weighed and examined. The nurse un-swaddled him, and Warner began to cry. I sweetly told him he was fine and put my right index finger into his hand, which he grabbed ever so tightly and immediately stopped crying! That was it. I was hooked! This was my pride and joy, and I was finally a father. I couldn't believe God's miracle that was given to us. Five pounds and five ounces and the sweetest smile in the world.

A few minutes later, I brought him back to the room and gave him to Tracy. The way Warner looked at his mom was unlike any I have ever seen. They were in love! I quietly wept with tears of pure happiness and joy. Our little family was finally complete.

The next day, Tracy's co-workers brought up some clothes and installed the car seat into Tracy's Saturn. Warner spent most of the day with us in our private room, except when he was with the nurses learning to feed out of the bottle. It took a while, but he finally started to get the hang of it. We were then told we would take him home the next day. We were both excited and scared at the same time! What if he cried and we couldn't get him to stop? What if he didn't sleep? What if? Many thoughts raced through our minds.

On Saturday, we brought him home on a very cold December afternoon. I drove like an old grandpa as I was making sure I didn't take any turns too fast to make his head shake! He was comfortable in his car seat, which helped later! We finally arrived home and as we brought him into the house for the first time, Lilly greeted us and was curious what this little thing was. When Tracy sat on the couch holding Warner, Lilly turned her head from side to side and wondered what in the heck this thing was!

We placed him in the bassinet and he immediately starting crying. Nothing helped besides holding him, but we needed him to sleep. That first night, none of us slept at all. Changing diapers, feeding and burping him... nothing worked! What did we get ourselves into? We all needed sleep, but that was soon to come.

On Sunday morning, we put him in his car seat to take him to the pediatrician for his first appointment. As soon as we backed out of the driveway, there was silence... he was sleeping! We enjoyed the thirty-minute ride while we dreamed of getting sleep. But having sweet dreams wasn't going to happen if Warner didn't sleep.

After we arrived at the doctor's office and talked to another couple, we were excited to learn that their baby only slept in their car seat, which came out of the holder in the car. We decided to give that a try. When we got home a few hours later, we took the car seat out of the car and put in the bassinet. He didn't make a sound! Halleluiah! We had solved the puzzle... the car seat was his new bed, at least for a little while!

A month after Warner was born, Lilly had another seizure, and I took her to the emergency vet. She was in bad shape and had developed terrible pancreatitis. I asked the vet if she was in pain, and she nodded yes. I had to make the toughest decision I ever made. I had to stop the suffering and put her down. I called Tracy and told her the news. She immediately came to be with me. Meanwhile, I held Lilly for the last time as they injected the fluids into her to stop her heart. My baby girl was gone! I thanked the vet and as I exited the front door, Tracy pulled up. I couldn't hide my hurt any longer and buried my head in her shoulder. I wept like a baby! I was heartbroken. Tracy consoled me, but it didn't help the hurt. However, the one thing I realized was that Lilly was no longer suffering and deserved to go with dignity! I felt I had made the right choice for her.

As the years and months passed us by, Warner was getting bigger and developing his own little personality. I was able to work my own business from home, so for the first five plus years, I basically took care of him. Feeding him, changing some nasty diapers, and, of course, playing with him. He was the cutest little boy and loved everyone he met. However, our family faced our biggest hurdle to date.

In May 2013, Tracy had a D&C done and two days later on Thursday May 9th, her OBGYN called her in to give her the news no one wanted to hear... you have cancer! Eight days later, she had a complete hysterectomy. The surgery lasted longer than expected. The doctor came out in the waiting room while I was with Janet, Shelly and Janet's pastor, Bruce. He pulled us aside and told us that she was in bad shape. Utter complete shock and heartbreak filled me. When she was brought to her room, she woke up and asked if she indeed had cancer, and I told her yes.

Without missing a beat, she said, "Well, it looks like I am going to have to kick cancer's ass!" Mind you, she never cusses, so it must have been the medicine!

The next Wednesday, Tracy and I went to South Carolina Oncology Associates to meet Dr. Williams and her staff to get the final prognosis.

"Tracy, you have stage 4 uterine cancer, and the death rate is about 80%" the doctor explained."

Once again, without missing a beat, my wife, who has terrible Math skills, said, "Well, Dr. Willams, if my math is correct, I have a 20% chance to survive, and to be honest, if I have at least a 1% chance, I am going to beat this and be here for my son!"

As I looked across the room, I saw shocked looks on the doctors and nurses faces... except for my Tracy! She was determined to beat this dreaded cancer.

The next six months were hell for Tracy as she went through extensive chemo. I had to face the reality that I might lose her. Warner was only three at the time and would rub Tracy's bald head all the time.

When Tracy would get sick, Warner would pat his mommy on the back and say, "Good job, Mommy. Get it out!" Such a sweet boy!

In early November, after 6 months of chemo, we heard the good news

"You are now cancer free!" She had done it, not that I was surprised because my wife is a true fighter and has been throughout her entire life! The pride she carries as a true cancer survivor still inspires to me. When you are down, you fight until God takes you!

In 2016, entering the first grade, Warner started attending Northside Christian Academy in Lexington. It was a small school that was very nurturing where he could learn about his faith. He thrived there and had some of the best teachers in Ms. Blake, Ms. Cruz, Ms. Jeffrey and Ms. Coulter.

While in the third grade, under the tutelage of Ms. Cruz, Warner made the decision that I am most proud of today. On Thanksgiving night, while he was in the shower, he yelled for his mom. Tracy, of course, raced into the bathroom and yelled for me to come in. I came into a dripping wet child, weeping in his mother's arms.

"Dad, I just surrendered myself to Jesus!" I immediately grabbed him and held him close. I was so proud for him to be a true Christian at such a young age!

That next February, while in chapel at school, Warner was baptized. I wept like a baby, tears of happiness and relief. My son's salvation had been determined. No matter what happened, I would see him forever in Heaven. What a comforting thought! Part of my duty as a father was done but bringing him up right still required work. Little did I know what he would do a few years later that would save me.

THE POWER OF PRAYER!

My Son Saved Me

PART TWO

CHAPTER 5

DECEMBER 13, 2020

My 48th Birthday! Birthdays are supposed to be filled with laughter, celebration, and joy. It's supposed to be that way no matter how young and how old you are. Birthdays for me as a kid were special, but once I turned 13, the tide turned. No more parties, no more celebrations, just a card and you are done. I guess being born so close to Christmas is not the way to go. I feel for my son, Warner, who was born on December 10th. Tracy and I make it a point to make his birthday one where he will have great memories. Each and every birthday means another year lived on this earth and should be celebrated!

This particular birthday was not one of my best. My symptoms had started the week before. I had a small fever of 99.7 and I ached. I felt so bad I went to see my primary care physician on December 8th with what I thought was a bad sinus infection. The doctor also gave me a COVID test. Remarkably, the test came back negative. This was the point during the pandemic where cases were sharply increasing, and the severity was at its worst. In the state of South Carolina, especially in the vicinity of the capital city of Columbia, almost all the ICU beds were taken. It was very scary knowing that you might not get the attention you deserve if you were forced to the hospital with COVID symptoms.

I was not particularly scared to get COVID but watching the local and national news the previous two months did have me a little concerned. I had been working from home for the past two months, as I was a contractor for Randstad, and my current position was with Wells Fargo Estate Care Center Team. In that role, I dealt with Wells Fargo bankers who had relatives of deceased family members in their respective branches. As the months leading up to December came and went, I saw more and more death certificates with the major cause of death due to COVID. Talk about making it real!

I did not feel well enough to drive on my birthday, so I asked Tracy if she could bring home Tokyo Grill, my favorite fast-food hibachi restaurant. I love the way they make their teriyaki chicken, and I was salivating at the thought of having the teriyaki chicken and the hibachi steak, along with vegetables and fried rice. I was anticipating the taste as I was extremely hungry.

When Tracy returned from her errands, she had a box of food, but it was not from my favorite restaurant. I was livid.

"It's my birthday and I want Tokyo Grill." I screamed at her, "I am not going to eat this crap!"

It was not normal for me to act this way towards my wife. I made her visibly upset, and she headed towards the bedroom with tears rolling down her cheek. All I could think was "Great job, Matt! She got you food, and you fussed... shame on you!" To this day, I regret my birthday, as I should have been grateful that she stopped to get me hibachi food in the first place!

I went back upstairs to my bonus room/office, which had a full-sized bed. I had been sleeping there for about five days because Tracy didn't want me to give my sickness to the rest of the family. My bonus room was awesome, complete with Ohio State Football gear, including a life-sized Fathead of my favorite Buckeye of all time, Eddie George. I was in college when he won the Heisman Trophy in 1995, so I naturally followed his career into the NFL. My room also had Cal Ripken, Jr memorabilia as well as Washington Redskins and Washington Capitals gear.

As I got back to my man cave, I started to feel some soreness in my chest. The first thing I thought of was, "At least it is not COVID!" Little did I know what was about to take place.

THE POWER OF PRAYER!

CHAPTER 6

DECEMBER 15, 2020

Two days had passed since my 48th birthday, and to be honest, I was feeling awful. My temperature was over 100 and my fever would not break, even with alternating Tylenol and Advil every 4 hours. My mind was starting to get a little foggy. Heck, even trying to walk ten feet to the restroom was a chore on its own. I had not felt this bad since I contracted mononucleosis in the seventh grade and was home from school for almost three weeks. This, however, was much worse.

Tracy called my cellphone at approximately 10am and asked if my fever had broken overnight. As I explained how I felt, including some heaviness in my chest, she suggested I get another COVID test. She found a drive-thru testing site at Lexington Family Practice at Saluda Shoals in Lexington, about a mile from my son's school. All I had to do was get to Lexington by 1pm to line up and get my test taken. I was sort of hoping Tracy could drive me, as I was in no condition to drive. However, work got in the way, so I had to attempt the drive myself.

Let me set the scene for you... I had to drive my 2007 Toyota Camry east on Interstate 26 for approximately ten miles and arrive at one of the worst disasters ever created in South Carolina... MALFUNCTION JUNCTION! Driving east, 26 crossed with Interstate 20, but the area made no logical sense. It was a three-lane road and about a half mile before 20, it broke into five lanes, with the extreme right lane existing to Interstate 20 towards Augusta (this was the direction I was headed). The third and fourth lanes would continue on a sharp... and I mean a sharp right turn towards Charleston. However, getting in the fourth lane were cars heading to Interstate 20 East towards Florence. All I have to say is whoever invented this mess of a junction must have been legally drunk at the time.

All I could do was pray as I attempted the drive. As I approached the Interstate 20-26 merge, traffic became increasingly heavy, with many cars swerving across two lanes. I was in the third lane and had a quarter of a mile to get in the far-right lane. I slowly worked my way over to the right lane and safely exited Interstate 26. As I merged onto Interstate 20 West, I started feeling dizzy and disoriented. How was I going to make it another 3 miles to the exit? Was I going to fall asleep at the wheel? God, please let me make it safely!

I arrived at Saluda Shoals at approximately 12:00pm. The drive-thru clinic didn't start for another thirty-five minutes, so I parked the car next door at

Chili's restaurant and took a quick nap. As I dozed off to sleep, my head was still spinning from the stressful drive I had to endure. All of a sudden, I heard a loud HONK! I quickly opened my eyes and looked at the clock... it was 1:45pm! I somehow got myself composed and made my way to the long line of cars already wrapped around the office.

How many of you have had the COVID test? Not the take-home test but the one you receive where a nurse will stick the swab so far up your nose, you feel like part of your brain is being damaged? Yep, this was my second test in a week. My car was the last one in line. As I made my way to the nurses, I thanked them for being on the front lines and risking their lives to help others. Simple as this... all nurses rock! After the wonderful nurse administered the test, I was told the results would be back no later than Thursday. Of course, I thought nothing of it, as I was sure I didn't have COVID, probably just the flu.

I thanked the nurses once again for their sacrifices and proceeded to head home. In a matter of seconds, I was home and in the driveway. WAIT A MINUTE! How did I get home? I had no recollection of the drive., How did I make it? I said a quick prayer and thanked God I made it some safely. I got in the house, went straight upstairs and dove right into bed. It took me no longer than a minute to fall asleep, and sleep I did! The next thing I knew, it was Wednesday morning. Why is time going by so quickly??

I made a call to Tracy downstairs, and she brought up some scrambled eggs and Gatorade. I thought I had the flu, so time to stay hydrated... nothing better than Gatorade! Tracy, however, dropped the plate and Gatorade on top of the mini-fridge at the door, a safe 20 feet away from the bed.

She told me she loved me and started walking, but I stopped her and asked, "Tracy, do you think I have COVID?"

She paused and nodded her head, then explained what she had just seen on the local morning news... all ICU beds in Columbia hospitals were taken. She was praying I didn't have it, but if I did, it would be hard to get treated.

The rest of Wednesday was tough with a ton of coughing... maybe it was bronchitis? I didn't sleep well Wednesday night, so I watched the NFL Network for most of it. I fell asleep around 4am or so, and when I woke up, my dog Zoe was in my face saying hello! She had always been by my side when I slept, so it was good to have a snuggle partner, but I missed Tracy and Warner.

Thursday afternoon arrived, and I was still feeling terrible as my temperature was rising to 101.5 and 102. My phone rang and my primary care physician told me the disturbing news... I tested positive for COVID! My heart sank, and I began to weep. I immediately called Tracy, who was downstairs with Warner, and told her the bad news.

I heard Warner scream, "Daddy can't die!"

Tracy decided she needed to get me to the hospital. As not to alarm Warner, she drove me to the Food Lion a mile from our house and called for an ambulance.

When the EMS crew arrived, Tracy told them the situation. One of the paramedics came to my side of the car and put an oximeter on my left index finger and sighed.

"Ma'am, we can't take him to the hospital. His oxygen level is at 81, and we can only take patients at Prisma with oxygen below 80. Tracy pleaded with the paramedics, but they talked for a few minutes and then drove off. My wife was not happy.

"Don't worry, honey. We will get you to a hospital in the morning. Let me make a few phone calls!"

We arrived back at the house. I gently went up the stairs and plopped on the bed. I said a quick prayer for some help, as it was getting harder to breathe. I got under the covers and went to sleep. What would tomorrow bring?

THE POWER OF PRAYER!

CHAPTER 7

DECEMBER 18, 2020

I didn't sleep well that night. Being turned away by the EMS really had me shaking. For the first time in my life, I didn't know if I was going to be alive much longer. The air was far less scarce than it was the day before. My chest hurt as I coughed, and my breathing labored. I could not taste the ice-cold Gatorade that I was drinking. I hadn't eaten in three days. Needless to say, I had not felt this bad in my entire life.

Tracy was on the phone making calls to medical personnel, who were also family friends. She was consulting with an infectious disease doctor, a pulmonologist and a triage nurse, explaining how I was feeling and how low my oxygen saturation rate was getting. That night, a neighbor went to Walgreen's to get an oximeter (which to this day I am so thankful for), and Tracy had me check it several times until it reached around 75%.

For some odd reason, I took a picture of myself

with eyes full of redness and puffed out with my goatee turning into a full-blown beard. When I looked back at that picture later, I wondered what in the heck was I doing taking a picture of myself at 3:40 am? Was I chronicling my last day on earth? Did I think I was going to die? To this day, no logical explanation makes sense as to why, in the middle of the night, full-blown COVID, I needed to take a selfie... geez!

Panic started to take form in all of us. We had no idea what was going to happen, and we were all worried. Warner, who had just turned 11, was concerned for his daddy. COVID has taken over my body and he was scared to come upstairs door to take a look. Like any other kid, he was curious but not brave enough to talk to me since my diagnosis had been confirmed the day before. He just wanted his daddy to come downstairs and play with him, you know, something normal!

Tracy called my cell phone several times throughout the night, but I said I was tired of checking my oxygen. I was beyond exhaustion and just wanted to sleep! Tracy was persistent. I have to give her credit; she would not take no for an answer. Tracy had possessed this trait through the first twenty-one years of marriage, and the Lord willing, she wasn't going to stop now.

Tracy has always been strong-willed and one of my favorite stories about her took place in the Dallas, Texas area, where she grew up. When she was about seven, she asked her parents if she could get a pool. It was all kids' dream to have their own pool. I had one growing up, and let me tell you, it was awesome. All your friends wanted to come over and hang with you. Summers for me were a blast! Well, Tracy deserved one.

When she questioned, he responded with, "If you dig the hole, I will fill it up for you!" Being just seven years old, she believed her father would stick true to his word. After all, her daddy was her life!!

What happened next were the beginning stages of Tracy being a leader. She went to all her friends' houses around the neighborhood, telling everyone to bring over anything they could find to dig a hole for this pool. Kids showed up with real spoons, forks, ice cream scoopers, wooden spoons, and even some shovels. Tracy drew up on paper the plans for the large pool, even with an island in the middle for a swing set. Tracy's mom came out and could not believe what she was seeing... fifteen kids scooping out grass and dirt, tossing it to the side and digging huge holes in the earth. Lesson learned... if you tell Tracy something, you better live up to your word. Tracy's father never filled in that hole with concrete and pool water. To this day, Tracy wants her own pool. It is my mission to get this for her sometime soon. I've just gotta figure out how many friends with spoons I need to dig that giant hole!

Even though it didn't work in her favor when she was seven, Tracy never gave up her persistent nature when she knew in her heart what was best. And she surely wasn't going to take no for an answer when my life depended on it.

The next thing I knew, Tracy was at the top of the stairs. "Matthew," she said, "I have the EMS here, and they are going to take you to Lexington Medical Center. Can you get out of the bed?"

At this point, I was not prepared to rise. My energy level was depleted, but deep down, I knew I had to make it out of that room. With everything I had, I got myself up and exited the room.

A very tall paramedic greeted me outside the door. "Mr. Shores, we are going to help you. Can you walk down the stairs by yourself?" I laughed for the first time in a week and made a sarcastic comment. The paramedic said, "Don't worry, Mr. Shores, I will hold on to the back of you so we can get you down the stairs and into the ambulance."

As I made the sixteen-step journey down the stairs, I noticed Tracy and Warner were gathered to see me race down the stairs... ha, more like a five-minute walk down the stairs!

Once I reached the last step, I sat down, and the paramedic put the oximeter on me. A few seconds later, I heard him yell, "We need oxygen now! This man is at 50% saturation!"

Within seconds, the second paramedic came with a stretcher and an oxygen mask.

As I made my way onto the stretcher, I heard Warner say, "I love you, Daddy. You are going to be just fine!"

I smiled as much as I could and told Warner, "Don't worry. I will come home soon."

The paramedic immediately put the oxygen mask

on so I could breathe. Within minutes, I was whisked away and the twenty-minute drive to the hospital commenced.

When we arrived at Lexington Medical Center, I was taken to an overflow area because all the beds in the ICU were taken.

"Don't worry, Mr. Shores," the nurse said, "We are going to take good care of you and get you back to your family. Now, Mr. Shores, do you have a living will, and if not, would you like to make one now?"

"There is no need for that," I explained. "I am going home in a day or two!"

The nurse started an IV and drew some blood. I also had a chest x-ray performed with a portable x-ray machine, so I didn't have to leave my bed. Technology has come so far, especially in the medical profession. I felt a sense of calm as the nurse attended to my every need. I felt so relaxed. I must have fallen asleep or not remembered the rest of that day.

On Saturday morning, a bed finally opened up in the COVID ICU Unit. I remember being wheeled into my room and being introduced to Dr. Philip Keith.

Dr. Keith took one look at me and said, "Sir, we are going to get you better and send you home to your family. That is my promise to you!"

"Dr. Keith, am I in danger of dying?" I asked reluctantly.

"Mr. Shores, you are in bad shape, but I am going to do everything possible to make sure you leave alive and free of COVID!"

At this point, I suddenly realized the situation I was

facing. Many questions raced through my mind. Was I going to live and see my family again? Would I go to heaven and see my family, who had passed before me? At that moment, I quietly said the Lord's Prayer to myself and gave all my worries to God. One thing was for sure, I needed some prayers. Do you believe in the power of prayer? I sure do!

The next three days were sort of a blur. I remember bits and pieces of what took place, but after looking at my online chart, I saw a few interesting things that took place that I have no recollection of. For example, I unhooked the catheter and told the nurse I wanted to eat it because it smelled like watermelon! I also pulled out IVs put into my arm. I hated things sticking out of me. A person in their right mind would keep the IVs in, but not me. I had no clue what I was doing, but the hospital staff was getting pretty fed up with my antics. How could I be such a terrible patient?

I had been in the hospital for several previous stays, extending from an emergency appendectomy in May 1997 to a kidney and UPJ stricture surgery in October 2013. I was always respectful, followed orders and had been a good patient. Why was I acting like a jerk? Apparently, COVID does that to some people, and I was one of them.

The biggest thing I did that scared the nurses and doctors was during a plasma infusion into my neck. Apparently, this plasma infusion was supposed to flush out the bad blood cells and infuse plasma into my bloodstream to head off the worst parts of COVID. What did I do instead? Without my knowledge, I ripped out the tubes attached to my neck, causing blood to get all over the bed. I didn't know until later that this was a huge no-no! Nurses and doctors rushed to suture me back up and prevent further bleeding. Thank goodness, they were so alert and on top of things! Nurses sure don't get the credit they deserve.

My mom was an awesome nurse. She would come home at night from Shady Grove Hospital in Rockville, Maryland, and tell stories about her day while we all had family dinner. Sometimes, she liked to give detail, and sometimes those details were very graphic, involving patients she had seen in the ER that day. Most people, including me, didn't like to hear the 'blood and guts' stories she would tell, but after a while I got used to it. She was so passionate about being a nurse, helping bring people back to life. She later worked in ICU and CCU, where her genuine care for her patients shined through. My mom had great compassion for her patients and their families, but working in the ICU was tough for her as she would lose patients all the time. She would come home those days and while talking at the dinner table, would shed tears because she was so sad to lose an old man whom she held hands with as they passed. My mom was amazing and her true love for others shined when she talked about her patients as if she knew their entire life story. I admired my mom for what she did. Nurses truly do care about their patients but are underpaid and overworked. I can say for a fact that I respect all nurses. They have to deal with a lot, so to all the nurses out there... THANK YOU!

Looking back at the nurses who dealt with me during my first few days of my hospital stay in the ICU, I can only say thank you! I know I was a royal pain and didn't act well, but please know that wasn't the true me. I was a very sick man, and I don't remember a lot about my first three days except for what I read afterwards in the patient portal, but you all were wonderful.

Meanwhile, at home, Tracy was not receiving frequent updates about my condition due to severe overcrowding. This became stressful for my wife and my son. Understandably, there we beside themselves with worry and fear. Little did Tracy know that the worst was yet to come.

THE POWER OF PRAYER!

Chapter 8

DECMBER 21, 2020

It was a very cold and dreary day in South Carolina. For my wife Tracy, days had passed since she had seen me and had been in constant contact with my closest friends, my dad and my brother, and also my wife's family in Texas. As each day passed, my condition worsened.

Sometime in the early afternoon, the phone rang in our Chapin home. Tracy answered reluctantly. No one fully understood or comprehended how badly I was doing until the doctors called and said...

"Mrs. Shores, your husband's condition has rapidly deteriorated. The only option now to try to save his life is putting him on a ventilator. This is probably one of the worst cases we have seen here since the pandemic started. The prognosis is not good as this is a last resort, but Mrs. Shores, you might want to prepare for the worst. He probably won't be alive for long."

My wife responded, "Dr. Keith, I assume you will have to put him under before you put my husband on the ventilator. I just want to warn you that Matthew is very difficult to knock out. He has woken up during several oral surgeries, Achilles surgery, and during an endoscopy. Trust me when I tell you that you will have to give him lots of medicine to get him sedated."

"We understand, Mrs. Shores," Dr Keith reluctantly agreed. "We do this all the time. I will let you know once he is fully intubated. Mrs. Shores, I hate to tell you this, but you might want to start making final arrangements, as the situation is dire. He probably won't be able to pull through."

Tracy hung up the phone and turned around to see Warner with a very concerned look on his face. "Mom, what is going on with Dad?" he asked.

Tracy, not wanting to hide anything from Warner, told him everything she heard from the doctor. Warner was so shocked that he started sobbing and mumbling, "I can't lose my dad. I need him here. What are we going to do, Mommy?"

"Sweetie, they will call once he is put on the ventilator and then all we can do is pray for Daddy."

My son sat in Tracy's lap, and they cried together. Was a phone call coming after intubation going to be the phone call with the devastating news? I can't imagine the fear and anxiety my wife and son were feeling, but Tracy knew that once they got the call I was intubated, they would reach out to many asking for prayers.

Hours later, the phone rang, and when Tracy answered she heard Dr. Keith's voice, "Tracy, you were right, we don't have him sedated and intubated yet. He *is* a hard one to knock out! We have given him the medicines we give to other patients, but he is still awake. We will continue to try to get him sedated, but since it is late at night, we will call you in the morning."

The next morning, Tracy heard from the hospital. "Mrs. Shores, we finally have your husband intubated, and he is on the ventilator. We gave him enough meds to kill a horse. He was a tough one to get under. You might want to start making arrangements, as we told you yesterday. This is only used as a last resort."

When Tracy hung up the phone, she immediately reached out to my four closest friends, my brother, my two closest cousins, and her closest family members. "We need to pray for him now. We can't lose him! Spread the word! I will keep you updated."

What happened next is what I truly believed started my healing. My son, decided to pray out loud, but this time to a special someone.

"God, I know I asked for a lot of things for Christmas. But to be honest, my dad is very sick with COVID and might die. God, I don't want a single present brought to me on Christmas morning. My Christmas wish is to have my dad alive and off the ventilator by Christmas Day. That is my Christmas wish. I know you can do it, so I am counting on you. I need my dad home with me... Amen!"

Tracy immediately hugged Warner, telling him how proud she was to have such a wonderful son. They both shed tears and knew they would get updates from the hospital every morning and night unless something happened. To this day, I cannot imagine the fear and anxiety they felt. Once word spread around our church, Salem United Methodist Church, families called and brought plates and plates of food for Tracy and Warner to eat. From what I gathered, they didn't have to cook a single meal until mid-January. As I look back on it, I am amazed at the true care that not only church family provided but also neighbors and friends showed as well.

Meanwhile, on Facebook, I had eight close friends who immediately posted pictures of me and them or pictures of my family, asking for prayers as I was fighting for my life! It started with:

Bobbi Ewin Prescott, a childhood friend since age 3.

Melinda Allman, a close friend from Montgomery College, whom I met in 1992.

Morgan Gelfound, whom I met in 1992 as a three-year-old, while hanging out with Melinda.

Coker classmates Karol Lowery Dixon, Pamela NeSmith Olson, Sharon Weresow, and Tanya Keith Kobylarz, along with staff member, Richard Carvajal.

After these eight beautiful souls posted, thousands upon thousands of replies were posted, staring with childhood friends from Maryland, those I knew from junior college, those from Coker College, those from my working days whether at Coker, First Citizens, Colonial Life and Wells Fargo. There were church friends, or people I knew outside of work, especially my fantasy football buddies who I had known most of them for twenty-plus years (Love you ACFL II group!). But it didn't stop there. There were at least hundreds up to thousands of replies from people I had never even met before. My COVID battle was being spread across all fifty states, and I later learned that prayer chains were even reaching Australia, Ireland, Scotland, Canada, Germany, Japan, and even parts of Africa and SE Asia. Tens of thousands of people across the globe were praying for me. And trust me when I tell you, I could feel all of their prayers. Prayers came from several religious and in many languages. It didn't matter if it was Christian, Jewish, or Islam, or if the prayers were said in English, Arabic, Japanese, or German. I was being uplifted for healing and for me to survive!

As I look back now at all the messages on Facebook that started from my initial eight friends on December 22, 2020, I continue to be amazed and downright humbled that so many took time to lift me and my family up in prayer.

As the next few days passed, more and more posts were on my Facebook feed, and even reading them now is actually a little overwhelming. Why me? What was so special about my situation? I was and still am an ordinary guy who happened to contract COVID and still people across these United States, as well as in foreign countries, lifted me up and thought enough to pray for me... THE POWER OF PRAYER!

While I was on the ventilator, I had many thoughts racing through my mind that I clearly remember. In my mind was a vision of a neighbor's sloped circular driveway shaped like a short two-way basketball court, and I watched LeBron James, Kobe Bryant, Shaquille O'Neal and Michael Jordan, among others, play pickup basketball, running back and forth like a classic NBA All-Star Game. This lasted for hours! I also had recollections of our trip to the State Championships and also me playing tennis. I told you I have a love for sports!

Something else happened while I was intubated that is important to share. Pay close attention to this part. Suddenly, I was in this dimly lit room, with no end in sight. There was a beautiful white light in the corner shining onto me, and for a few moments, I didn't know where I was. I struggled to see what was ahead of me. It was a little foggy and hazy, so I couldn't see the floor. As I looked out in the distance, I noticed someone walking towards me.

The figure was walking rather briskly and as it got closer and closer, I heard a voice say, "There's my baby!" IT WAS MY MOTHER! "Hey there baby," she spoke as she got closer to me.

Her face was radiant like the sun, her hair perfect and waving in the air. She walked towards me and once she reached me; she gave me a kiss on my forehead, and I could actually feel her moist lips.

"Mom, what is going on? Is this heaven?" I asked.

"Matthew, we don't have much time to talk. First, I want to tell you that I am so proud of you and what you have made of your life. Your wife is awesome, and I loved her from the start. I see my grandson every day and pray for him often. You have raised a great young man."

"Mom, I don't understand. Why am I here?" I asked.

"Son, I have a message to pass along to you. You are

not supposed to be here. It is not your time yet. You need to go back and take care of Tracy and Warner. They still need you, and you need to be with them for a long time. But you have to promise me something. Whatever obstacles you face, son, you cannot give up. You must fight and get better! Hear me, son, you must fight! Promise me!"

"I promise Mom! I miss you!" I wept with my hands on my face.

"I miss you too, baby, but you need to go back now. You made a promise, so stick to it, no matter what lies ahead of you... fight, fight, fight!"

She started to walk away, and I yelled, "Mom, Mom, please come back. Mom, Mom."

The next thing I knew, I felt a real sensation of something being taken out of my throat. Then I heard a voice say "Matt, Matt"

"Mom, is that you?" I asked.

"No Matt, it's Doctor Keith. Can you open your eyes?"

I struggled for a few moments, but as I slowly opened my eyes, I saw a tall man and three others dressed in yellow, with huge masks over their heads. I didn't have my glasses on, but I could make out the figures somewhat.

"Matt, I can't believe you made it back. You put up a heck of a fight. You are our Christmas miracle!"

THE POWER OF PRAYER!

CHAPTER 9

DECEMBER 25, 2020

Christmas morning! It is the moment a lot of people look forward to, especially children, as they can't wait to open gifts from Santa. Years earlier, my son thought he heard Santa in the house while in the room with my mother-in-law, whom he calls Mia.

It was 2am, and he rushed into our room and yelled, "Mommy, Daddy, Santa was here, come see!" Tracy and I both gave each other a 'What is he thinking' look. After much deliberation, we got up and watched him quickly opened his presents. At 3am, we went back to sleep while Warner played with his new toys... ah, to be a kid again!

This Christmas morning was much different. Tracy and Warner tried to rest as sleep deprivation was kicking in. For days, they had been worried about my condition and didn't want to hear that the news everyone feared.

The phone then rang. Warner picked up the phone,

saw on Caller ID that it was Lexington Medical Center, and immediately yelled for Tracy to answer. She reluctantly answered and stayed silent for a minute. Warner was, of course, trying to figure out the conversation while reading Tracy's face.

After that minute, Tracy said, "Could you please repeat that?" as a shocked look came over her face. Not a minute later, she said thank you and hung up. She turned to Warner and said, "You are not going to believe this, but your daddy is off the ventilator and is doing fine." My son then shifted his heads upwards, looking towards the heavens and said, "My Christmas wish came true...thank you, God!"

Tracy immediately called her inner circle and told them all to spread the good news. I was alive, and I was a Christmas miracle! As news spread, Facebook lit up with great news about my current condition, but I wasn't out of the woods yet. A lot of fighting still had to be done.

After seeing Dr. Keith, I don't remember much about the next two days. I was still very drugged from all the medications it took to sedate me, but I vividly remember being in a hospital bed in a closed room with nothing around me. I was scared and started to scream for help.

"Help me, help me," I screamed at the top of my lungs. "Where am I? Please come help me and tell me what is going on." I continued to scream for what seemed like hours, pressing every red button on my bed, but no one came. I started to wonder if I was really alive. Nothing in my room looked familiar. All I could see was a mirror on the wall at the foot of the bed. After what seemed like an eternity, a doctor came in and assured me I was fine and to keep my voice down. "What am I doing here?" I confusedly asked. "What is going on?" The doctor assured me that I was in Lexington Medical Center with COVID. He told me to remain calm as they were taking good care of me, and I needed to get some rest.

What seemed like an instant but was probably a day later, I awoke to find a male nurse in my room who was drawing blood and changing out my IV fluids. I asked his name, which of course I forgot ten seconds later, so I asked again. The nurse assured me that my memory was going to be foggy and unstable, and he asked me to please not take out my IV. I learned later when I returned home that I had attempted to pull the IV tubes out of my arm before a nurse stopped me. No wonder every time a new nurse came over the next week, I heard, "Mr. Shores, please don't pull on your IV's." At that time, I didn't know any better.

The nurse pushed the button on the bed to lift my head up some, and I asked for my glasses. I wanted to be able to see everything around me. After I was given my glasses, I looked towards the right and on the table was my son's 3rd grade football picture in a frame. The nurse told me that my family wanted to me have things in my room to remember them by. I cried and told the nurse I wanted to go home. I wanted to see Tracy and Warner. I then heard the news that gave me a sense of reality.

"Mr. Shores, you came off the ventilator yesterday

and are still sick with COVID. That is why I am wearing this protective gear to keep us safe and protected. You have a long road ahead of you, but I know you are going to make it out of here if you continue to fight!"

"Do you see that picture?" I asked, "That is my son, Warner, and he is 11. He is my everything. I need to see him, but I promise to listen to you all so I can get home as quickly as possible. He and my wife are everything to me, and I will do anything to get better and get out of here. When can I leave?"

"Mr. Shores, it is going to take a long time for you to recover, so we are going to take good care of you and make sure you see your wife and son again. This is going to be a marathon, not a sprint home!"

He gave me a cup of ice chips and I quickly sucked on them and swallowed, enjoying the wetness of the ice melting in my mouth. It felt so good! I then noticed the catheter that stretched into a large bag on the side of the bed as he was emptying out my fluids.

"Whenever you feel like you have to poop, please do so in this." He handed me a metal pan. I asked what it was and was told it was a bedpan. I thought to myself, with my bathroom inhibition, no way was I pooping into it.

"I am going to get up and poop!" The nurse laughed and said sure, so I thought I was getting out of bed, but was hallucinating as I was flying down the hallway into the bathroom and then flew back and told him, "Done!"

He looked at my bedpan, laughed and said there

was nothing there. I told him I went down the hall to poop and he laughed again, telling me I hadn't moved an inch. It felt so real to me, but the nurse assured me I was hallucinating due to all the meds administered to sedate me. I shook my head in disbelief. It all seemed real to me. Why not to him?

For the next three days, I slept well and started to have a liquid diet, which I tolerated well and was so excited when I graduated to real food. Finally, no more chicken broth or ice chips., I must say that the three portions I got every day were very plentiful and tasty. I started to think to myself I could get used to this. I have always loved food, even when I was skinny. In 2003, I started to gain weight rapidly. When I got married in 1999, I weighed 150 pounds, but four years later I had ballooned to 270 pounds! That is a lot of weight to gain in just a four-year period. I had tried Weight Watchers when working for First Citizens.

One of my favorite co-workers told me one day when I was very grumpy, "Matt, just eat a cheeseburger and stop being so fussy!" I will forever remember that line my cubemate said to me, as she along with others were done with my low-calorie diet and the grumpy attitude I had.

Every morning a nurse would walk into my room, introduce themselves and ask if I knew the date, which I recited, and then asked me why I was there, to which I responded, "I have COVID!"

"Great, your memory is starting to improve. Keep it up Mr. Shores."

One morning, I met my favorite nurse named Lisa.

I know you aren't supposed to have favorites, but she was mine. She came in with such positive energy. She held my hand and gently asked how I was doing. I told her I was ready to go home, and she assured me that if I continued improving, it wouldn't be long.

Lisa had been a nurse for over thirty years and was so caring. Her voice, however, was very distinct and sounded like my mom's sister, my Aunt Joyce, who was also a nurse but passed away several years before. My Aunt has a very distinct and unique voice, but Lisa's was almost the same! As she stayed in my room for most of her twelve-hour shift, I could feel the presence of my Aunt Joyce through Lisa. It's almost like God placed her there to remind me that my family was there to support me.

That day, Lisa had decided that the catheter needed to come out and that I needed to pee in the large urinal container so I could start to do things on my own. For the first time, she led me out of bed into a recliner positioned to the left of my bed. Wow, it felt good to get up and take three tiny steps to the recliner. This took several minutes and by then my breathing was labored. Lisa assured me it would take a while to get used to walking again and to regain my strength due to the virus. She sat me in the recliner with my feet up and put two different breathing machines by my side on the table. One was for me to blow in to get my lungs to expand. This was the easy one, as I did it repeatedly for several hours. The other one was tough. I had to take in air and the device went upward in pressure as I took in more air. I am telling you what, this took me weeks to master but was so vital in my recovery.

For the next two days, I was ready every morning for the nurse to help me out of bed and into the recliner, which I spent most of the day in, talking to other nurses, aides and the doctors who checked on me all the time. Dr Keith was the main doctor in the ICU who specialized in COVID. He visited me every morning and before he left at night. Each night, he would take his tablet and have me face time with Tracy and Warner. What an emotional time that was. I was still slurring most of my words, but I was thrilled to see my wife and my son's face to face. I enjoyed every short five-minute conversation with those two. It made my day and my recovery much more meaningful.

What remained, though, were the hallucinations. From me imagining I was sitting at the nurse's station eating chocolate to visiting other patients in the COVID wing and even getting up a lot to go to the window and look across to another room with and old patient and her daughter, the hallucinations kept coming. I told this to Dr. Keith, who reminded me that I might still have hallucinations for a few more days, but little did I know that soon I would have one that would change the course of my recovery.

THE POWER OF PRAYER!

CHAPTER 10

DECEMBER 31, 2020

I woke up very early on New Year's Eve. My cell phone had been by my table, but I hadn't used it at all, so once the nurse gave me a charger, I called Tracy. It must have been 5am and I am sure I woke her.

"What are you thinking? It's still dark!"

I just wanted to talk to my wife but was politely told that she needed to sleep and so did I. Only one of the few times my wife has deliberately hung up on me.

At the start of the 7am shift, I waited in eager anticipation to meet my nurse for the day, but also for breakfast. I was starving! A few minutes later, my nurse walked in and introduced herself. To this day, I don't remember her name. She was so cheerful and happy to be at work. She started off with my meds, trying to rip open individual packages of pills while having gloves on. I have no clue how nurses managed that. I would be using scissors or breaking protocol by taking my gloves off and tearing them, thereby risking myself to COVID exposure.

"We are off and running like a herd of turtles!" my nurse proudly exclaimed.

I told the nurse that I have heard that phrase from one other person... my wife Tracy! She used it all the time as she would leave for work in the morning or while we would get in the car to go on a trip. It was one of many of my wife's catchphrases, the favorite one being "Sap Sucking Son of a Siberian Sheepgoat!" You see, my wife, up to that point, had only cussed twice in front of me. The first was the night she delivered our son, and the other was when she was diagnosed with stage 4 uterine cancer in May 2013. Besides these two instances, she uses her very colorful but unique sayings. Gosh, I love my wife!

Anyway, the nurse laughed and found it funny that other people used her catchphrase. She gave me my meds and some water, then we talked for a good while about who was in the picture and about my family. I was starting to get most of my bearings back but was still uneasy. After breakfast, the nurse led me to my recliner and left for a bit. I had to go to the bathroom, so I took the urinal hand container and proceeded to pee like there was no tomorrow, almost filling the large container. As I reached to put on the table, it moved, and the urinal fell onto the floor and my urine spilled everywhere.

"What in the hell happened?" my nurse yelled at me. "How can you be so clumsy? Now I have to clean this up!" I apologized repeatedly, and the nurse left the room, disgusted. Several minutes later, a janitor came into my room, and I apologized repeatedly for spilling the urine, but was reassured that it was an accident. I still felt bad. I wondered why my nurse yelled at me so rudely. As I was starting to weep, the dietician came in and saw me crying. I explained what I had done, and even the dietician said I had no right to be yelled at like that. As I calmed down, I learned I had lost about 30 lbs., and they were concerned about my weight loss. Watching me woof down my lunch, the dietician said there was nothing wrong with my eating habits and I should be fine.

As she left, the physical therapist came in, a very charming lady in her early 60s, who greeted me and bowed just like a performer in a theatre. She was excited to teach me how to walk again, which I laughed at to begin with, but soon realized I had a long way to go. I got up, took two steps forward, turned and took two steps back to the recliner and sat down. I was out of air, panting and having labored breathing. In reality, I thought this took about one minute, but as I sat down, the physical therapist congratulated me on my fifteen-minute exercise. What? It took me fifteen minutes to walk four total steps.

"I will be back tomorrow to continue working with you and have a nice day." She once again bowed, to which I gave her applause.

The nurse came back in with a scowled look on her face and handed me a pill and told me to take it. No more than a minute after I took the pill, I blacked out! Approximately four hours later, I woke up very groggy and unsure where I was. What had happened? Had someone forgotten about me? Why was I still in the recliner? Now is when some crazy stuff happened.

As I started to wake up a little more, I noticed that my ankles were attached to something. I couldn't move them, or so I thought. I looked to my left out of the glass door and saw another nurse and motioned for her to come in.

As she entered the room, she let out a gasp and said, "My gosh, what has she done now?"

The second nurse left and came back with what looked like a tool kit and started to work on my legs. As she was working, my original nurse popped in and yelled at the other nurse to leave. After she did, my morning nurse gave me a shot thru my IV. She told me it was Lasix, which would make me pee for hours, and this time I'd better not drop the urinal or else!

What was going on here? Was this neglect by my nurse? No more than ten minutes later, I felt the urge to pee. I immediately grabbed the urinal and proceeded to let loose for several minutes, mostly filling the container. I called for my nurse, who came and told me good job for not dropping it. She said she wanted to give me more Lasix.

I immediately screamed and was greeted with a hand over my mouth, then whispering, "One more word out of you, and you are done, get it?" She administered more Lasix and then swiftly left the room.

I had to do something. Was my nurse trying to harm me, or even take me out? I started to breathe heavily, and the next hour repeatedly relieved myself in another urinal container. I had to tell Dr. Keith, but how? I grabbed my cell phone and tried to unlock my it but couldn't remember the passcode. I was scared.

I yelled to my nurse, "I called the police on you!"

"No, you didn't!" she shouted, and then all hell broke loose. She darted into the room, took my phone and told me, "It's over!" She left the room, and I prayed. I prayed so hard that tears were flowing from my eyes. I feared for my life. Was she trying to kill me? What was I going to do? The next thing I knew, Dr. Keith came in and sat on the bed across from me.

"What's going on, Matt?" he asked, to which I explained that my nurse was trying to kill me. I asked Dr. Keith where he had been, and he told me he was intubating another patient who had COVID, just like he did to me. Three nurses suddenly entered the room, surrounding my chair. As I looked to my left out the glass door, nurses and hospital staff lined up the entire window. I thought to myself, this was the end. I was going to die! I tried to get up but was held down by one nurse with her kneecap on the top of my upper leg, causing instant pain.

"Matt, we are going to end this right now," said Dr Keith. Was this how my life was going to end? I attempted to get up once more, but the nurse put pressure on my leg again. I bowed my head, silently said a prayer, then looked at Dr. Keith and said, "If you do it, make it quick and painless."

The two other nurses led me to the bed and l looked out to the right towards the window. Dr. Keith was sitting down, and a nurse was mixing something up in what looked like a shot glass. I was freaking out. I told Dr Keith that I thought he was different.

"You know me, Matt," he responded, then injected the liquid into my IV. I looked up at the ceiling, knowing I was probably taking my final breath, and apologized out loud to Tracy for not coming home. As the seconds faded, my eyes were about to close. Was this the end?

THE POWER OF PRAYER

CHAPTER 11

JANUARY 1, 2021

Everything was dark. Where was I? Was on my way to heaven, or maybe to hell for some strange reason? I couldn't move my legs at all and could barely move my arms. What was going on? Why was it so quiet?

All of a sudden, I felt light, as if the sun had suddenly appeared similar to that of a solar eclipse. I struggled to look ahead of me, but within a minute my vision got clearer and believe it or not, I was in my hospital bed. A sense of relief came over me... I was alive! But where was everyone, and what day was it?

To my right, I heard a voice from a young woman with a Caribbean accent. I turned in that direction as was greeted by a nurse.

"Hello Mr. Shores, how are you feeling? You got some good rest, I see."

For some strange reason, my mind was very fresh, and I had my wits about me. The nurse told me it was 5am, and that I had slept through New Year's Eve and all the commotion in the ICU as the nurses celebrated the beginning of 2021. I looked down towards the end of the bed to see my ankles secure to the bed.

"Don't worry Mr. Shores, that was just a precaution from yesterday so you wouldn't get out of the bed and hurt yourself. I will take care of that for you." She unlatched the straps around my ankles, and I was finally free.

The nurse and I had a wonderful conversation that lasted approximately an hour. We talked about her coming to the states from the Bahamas, her studies to become a nurse, which fulfilled her parents' wishes, and our love for the Methodist Church and its founder, John Wesley and how he impacted so many lives around the world.

"Mr. Shores, I must tell you, I am surprised to see you like this! According to your chart, it seems as if the COVID affected most of your mental abilities. For example, you took out several IVs including the plasma infusion, you took out your catheter and tried to eat it, and some of the nurses noted you might have been hallucinating, especially last night."

I kept quiet about what I remembered from the night before, not willing to take any chances. What occurred the day before seemed so real? Did I really hallucinate?

"You are a pleasant man, Mr. Shores, and if you notice, your nurse left you a note on the board."

I struggled to make out the writing, but as my vison started to clear, I read aloud the message on the board. "I hope you feel better. You scared us all last night. I hope you had a good night's sleep and got some much-needed rest. Tracy and Warner called to wish you a Happy New Year and say they loved you."

I could not believe my eyes. Did the "wicked" nurse leave me a nice note? It was in the same handwriting used to write her name and info the day before on the nurse's board in my room. Maybe I did hallucinate that they were trying to harm me. How do I make this better? Random thoughts raced through my mind as I felt a touch on my right arm.

"Mr. Shores, I am going to let you be for a little. I get off in a few minutes, but I will be back to see you tonight at 7."

I nodded in approval and watched the nurse leave the room. I sat in disbelief for a few minutes until I noticed my cell phone beside me on the table. I picked it up and saw several text messages, notably from Tracy, my brother and two friends wishing me a Happy New Year and asking if I was going to be able to watch the big game tonight.

That's right, my beloved Ohio State Buckeyes were playing tonight in the Sugar Bowl against the Clemson Tigers in the College Football Playoff semifinal. Clemson had Ohio State's number when we played them the past three times we met in either a bowl game or the College Football Playoff. In fact, the year before, we played a great game against Clemson in the semifinal, with RB J.K. Dobbins running wild the first half, but Clemson QB Trevor Lawrence led the Tigers back to a late lead only to see our QB Justin Fields throw an interception into the end zone in the last thirty seconds as we tried to score to win the game. I remember being so disappointed in the outcome, yet so proud of how my Buckeyes played that year against the defending national champions. We weren't given a chance to win, and I believed that this year we would finish the job.

"Matthew, what are you still doing here?" a lady exclaimed and as I looked up, it was none other than my favorite nurse... Lisa! "I thought you would be long gone out of ICU by now. How have you been?"

As I started to talk, another familiar voice joined in, "Hey Mr. Shores, feeling better this morning?" It was Dr. Keith!

"Dr. Keith, I don't know what happened last night, but apparently, I was in the wrong, so I apologize. Can you please forgive me?" I pleaded, as if asking for my life back.

"Matt, there is nothing to apologize for. Whether you realize it or not, you did hallucinate last night, but I told you I was going to take care of you. I have studied COVID for almost nine months now, and you were one of the worst cases I have seen and survived. God has a plan for you. Just make sure to keep your eyes and ears open for him."

I gently nodded, and he handed me his tablet so I could say Good Morning to my family. I was so thrilled to see Warner's face pop up and greet me with his familiar, "Hello Daddy, I miss you!"

I started to weep a little as I realized that I was seeing my son again. We talked for a few minutes about how he tried to stay awake for the ball to drop, but both he and Mom fell asleep on the couch, but he was excited for the big game tonight.

"O-H," I said to him.

He excitedly responded, "I-." His hands and arms created the familiar sign. I was so proud of that moment that we got to share, realizing I had raised a true Buckeyes football fan!

I briefly talked to Tracy, who was visibly tired and needed some rest. "Get some rest honey, I am going to watch Ohio State win tonight, so say a prayer for a victory!"

She nodded and ended the call. Even though our contact lasted only thirty seconds, it did my heart good to see her and my son in 2021, which we never thought I would see. I was truly a walking, talking miracle!

Dr. Keth patted me on the back and said he would check on me often to make sure I was doing well. Once Dr. Keith left, I was brought my breakfast, which was one of my favorites… pancakes! I could taste every morsel of the yummy hotcakes with sausage and hash browns. It felt good to have all my bearings back, and I felt so alert and awake.

After breakfast, with Lisa's help, I got in the recliner.

"Matt, you look like you need a wash and a shave! Let's get you looking good for the New Year!" She got wet towels and wipes and proceeded to wash me from head to toe, which felt so good. She even washed my feet, which reminded me of Jesus when he washed his disciple's feet. Next, she took an electric razor and shaved my entire mustache and beard, which I admit had me looking ten years younger.

After the two-hour long wash and shave, Dr. Keith walked in and exclaimed, "Matt, you look like a new man! Let's take a picture!"

I handed him my phone, and he took a picture, which I immediately sent to Tracy.

She responded within seconds, saying, "Wow, you look different!"

Tracy had always loved my goatee but seemed to love my new look!

I looked at the picture and my first thought was, "Wow, you are truly a miracle! Let's live life like it from now on. A New Year and a new outlook on life."

Throughout the rest of the day, I contemplated whether to stay away for the entire CFP Semifinal. I began to get very tired as each hour passed. At 6:30pm, while watching the Alabama-Notre Dame Semifinal, Lisa came back in, gave me the biggest hug, and told me she would never forget me. I told her I would never forget her and the love and compassion she showed as a nurse. 'I felt a tear roll down my left cheek and she wiped it away, telling me I had come a long way. Then we prayed together for a minute before she left. That was the last time I would see Lisa, my favorite nurse of all time!

A little after 7pm, the same nurse from the night before came in and greeted me. I told her I was hope-fully going to be watching football, but she saw I was getting noticeably tired. Right before the game was about to start, I asked if I could be given my nighttime medication, which she happily gave me. There was no way I could stay awake for the whole game... little did I know what the next four hours would bring!

The Buckeyes got the ball, then went 3 and out, and then Clemson got an early score. Down 7-0 with only five minutes into the game and I suddenly felt depressed. I was about to turn off the TV and get to bed but decided to watch one more possession. What started as five minutes turned into about four hours of complete joy and excitement. QB Justin Fields had the game of his life. Six total touchdowns and 429 passing yards later, the Buckeyes has finally beaten Clemson by a score of 49-28. We had punched our ticket to the National Championship for the first time since 2015. I got so excited during the game that my nurse came in several times to calm me down as my heart rate and blood pressure skyrocketed.

It was after midnight when the game ended and, of course, I had to watch the postgame celebration with Coach Ryan Day and my beloved Buckeyes raising the Sugar Bowl trophy. It was a night I would never forget. I got many texts from my fantasy football group congratulating me on my big victory. Then reality hit me. How long would I be in the hospital, and would I have a slight chance of getting home before the January 11th Championship game? Suddenly, I felt a severe motivation to get home. I wanted to be with my wife and son.

THE POWER OF PRAYER!

CHAPTER 12

JANUARY 3, 2021

T his day started much earlier than anticipated. I woke up at approximately 4am to my two nurses coming into the room and turning the lights on.

"Good news Mr. Shores! You are leaving the ICU unit and headed to the step-down unit for COVID recovery!"

I could not believe what I was hearing. I was finally leaving the ICU! Don't get me wrong, I was excited to get in a real room but hated leaving the doctors and nurses I had formed a bond with, especially Dr. Keith and my favorite nurse, Lisa.

It took the nurses approximately thirty minutes to gather all the items from my closet and nightside stand. The next thing I knew, I was being helped into the wheelchair to be sent across the hospital. As I left my ICU room for the final time, I waved to all the staff and thanked them for taking good care of me, even though I had been a tough patient. The ICU doors opened, and we entered the elevator to go down two flights to hit the breezeway to the newest part of Lexington Medical Center. I was told that I was going to the ninth floor where COVID patients were recovering. Was I dreaming or hallucinating? Heck no, I was taking my next step in my COVID journey with the ultimate goal of getting home as quickly as possible.

As I entered the end of the ninth floor, I was wheeled into my new room, and what a spacious room it was. There was a huge couch on the far side with a view overlooking the skyline. On the right side of the bed was a very comfy recliner with blankets galore. I could already picture myself in the recliner watching TV while trying my best to recover. A huge bathroom was in there, and I was so excited to be able to use a real toilet rather than using a urinal container or bedpan. I felt like I had struck gold or won Powerball. That's how good it felt to be in new surroundings to further my recovery.

The two nurses unloaded my stuff and hooked my oxygen canula to the bedside oxygen wall plate. "Mr. Shores, it has been a pleasure, and we wish you nothing but the best. We hope you get to go home soon!"

I hugged them both, got into a very comfortable bed, and turned on the TV. I was making myself at home when my new nurse from the floor walked in and greeted me. My vitals were taken, and I was told to relax until the next shift arrived for my day nurse to take care of me.

A little after 7am, my nurse came in and introduced himself. He noticed I was watching NFL Network and commented he had been a longtime Bills fan. After I told him I was a fan of the Redskins, he chuckled and thanked me for handing his team the second of four consecutive Super Bowl losses in the early 90s. We chatted for a few minutes, and I was given my morning medication. After breakfast was delivered, he gave me a quick rundown on how this unit works and informed me that even though I was finally discharged from ICU; I had a long way to go in my recovery. I was told that every thirty minutes I was to work on the breathing machine that would help expand my lungs and get rid of the dreaded COVID.

The next few days went pretty well, and I was able to get some sleep during the night, but not as much as I needed. I knew I needed to get home to sleep in my own bed, where I would be totally comfortable. During those next three days, I worked hard on my breathing machine and could tell a difference in my lung capacity. A tech came in every day and took a chest x-ray with a portable machine, which I thought was the coolest invention ever!

Physical therapists came in three times daily and worked with me on learning to walk again, which I must say was very difficult and very draining. After a fifteen-minute session, I would get into bed and instantly fall asleep. Little did I know how draining getting over COVID was going to be.

The one thing I noticed was my growing need to talk to my son and my wife. I was getting homesick, and I mean homesick in the worst way possible. I wanted to go home so badly that I asked the morning nurse every day with no timetable given back to me. All I wanted was to be home to recover. I was sick and tired of being in the hospital with no visitors except hospital staff. I wanted to see familiar faces and give and get hugs from my loved ones. I felt very lonely and told my wife Tuesday night that I wanted to come home tomorrow. I was informed that they were going to keep there for a while, and I needed to remain patient. However, that was not possible. I needed my family, and I needed them now.

As I began to cry, Tracy consoled me and told me to hang in there and not to worry about when I was going to be released. Luckily, I had my cell phone, so I proceeded to get in contact with my close friends through text message to make time go by faster. I had a bug up my butt to get home ASAP and was bound and determined to make it happen.

Wednesday, January 6, 2021, was a day I will never forget. It started with a 4am phone call to my wife. She handed the phone to my son, who was more than willing to talk to his father. We chatted about wrestling and football and how much we missed each other. After a thirty-minute conversation, he told me that he needed some more rest, so I reluctantly let him go and decided to get some rest as well.

The nurse came in and administered my medications. After breakfast and physical therapy, I was wiped, and I fell asleep for many hours. When I woke up, I turned on the news and was shocked at what I was seeing.

President Trump was speaking to his supporters at

the White House and told the crowd, "Go take back what is yours!" He meant the US Capitol, and I learned that VP Pence was not going to overturn the election results. For the next two hours, I saw some things happen that scared me to death. A mob of people headed towards the Capitol, and they began to beat down officers and security and made their way past the barricades surrounding the building. The microphones following the crowd were very clear and once past security, they broke into the Capitol building chanting, "Kill Pelosi" and "Kill Pence." They were ransacking the US Capitol. Thousands of rioters were tearing the place apart, people shouting to find and kill members of Congress.

I was in total shock. I am not arguing politics here. This is not a political rant. But when a mob of people overrun and trample officers and security and then take down barricades and forcefully enter a closed Congressional building, demanding the killing of members of Congress and the Vice President... that is where I draw the line! I could not believe that the country I love so much had people rioting and wielding guns threatening to kill people. I believe in peaceful protest and the right to assemble, but not in a closed off setting. What took place reminded me of how divided a country we have become.

I called my wife, and we both watched on separate TVs as the events unfolded on a terrible day in our country's history. My wife told Warner that this type of action among citizens of our country is wrong and there are other avenues to take if you want to peacefully protest. We both shared how scared we were and agreed it was wrong. We decided to turn off coverage and switch to something happy. I expressed my urgent desire to go home, but the doctor and my wife agreed I wasn't ready... yet!

I spent Thursday on the phone for most of the day, talking to my wife and son, my friends Richard and Larry, and with my brother in California. I expressed my deep desire to get home quickly as I was done with hospital life. I so badly wanted to discharge myself, but I knew that wasn't the best thing to do for my recovery. During my downtime, I prayed to God to please let me go home. Little did I know that my wish was going to be granted soon, and when I say soon, I mean soon!

THE POWER OF PRAYER!

CHAPTER 13

JANUARY 8, 2021

I t was a cold and rainy morning at Lexington Medical Center as I peered out the window, looking over the Carolina winter skyline. I was tired, physically and emotionally! The past two days were spent with the nurses giving me Lasix, mainly to flush the toxins out of my body. It got some fluids out, but I didn't think it was enough. How long did I have to stay? I was lonely and desperate to get home!

My morning nurse walked in at 8am and silently approached my bed. She grabbed my left hand with her right hand, covered by a latex glove.

"Matt, I am going to tell you something." My heart sank into my stomach.

What bad news was coming next? A move to another room or worse news that I was staying for a much longer period of time than anticipated.

"How would you like to go home today?" she asked. What happened next was just a knee-jerk reaction.

I shouted at the top of my lungs, "YES!" All the

negative thoughts and emotions immediately left my conscience, and instant thoughts of Tracy and Warner danced in my head.

"First, we have to give you a little more Lasix and then, if things go well, we will discharge you at 3:30 today! How's that for good news?"

I pulled the nurse closer, gave her a big hug and told her thanks probably a million times. At that moment, the doctor came in and reinforced that if the Lasix worked well like they anticipated, I would be able to go home.

"Does my family know yet?" I asked.

I was told to call them and give them the good news, with instructions on where to be and when. I immediately picked up my cell phone and dialed my wife. Before she could get the entire traditional greeting of hello. I screamed, "I'm coming home today!"

"Are you sure, Matthew? Do the doctors and nurses think you are ready?" she asked.

I told her the rundown of the rest of the day and then the nurse told my wife where to come to pick me up that afternoon. I couldn't believe it... I was going home!

After I devoured my breakfast in record time, my nurse administered the Lasix, and within five minutes, I excreted 280 mL of urine. Flushed it down the toilet, got back to the recliner, and then excreted 270 mL, then 260 mL twice more within a thirty-minute span. I pressed the call button for the nurse station and told them the number of times going to the bathroom and the levels.

"Sounds like you and your body are excited to go home. Let's get your discharge papers ready and go over instructions on your oxygen usage for home."

I admit I was a little shocked. Why was I going home on oxygen? The nurse came in and explained that even though I was going home, I needed to be on oxygen for another six months! I was also told that I would follow up with a pulmonologist within the next ten days. Suddenly, my excitement turned into despair. Why did I have to be on oxygen at home for such a long time? How was I going to work upstairs on the phones for Wells Fargo? I couldn't make it up the stairs. How were we going to survive?

I had learned a month before my hospitalization that my goddaughter Gillian, who was finishing up her last year at Texas Tech, was getting married and the date had been set for July 5th. Suddenly, this intense motivation came over me that I was not going to miss her wedding. I was going to do everything in my power to defy the odds and get off oxygen much sooner than anticipated and to dance at my goddaughter's wedding in Texas. Besides my son and wife, I had another reason to continue fighting.

As the day progressed, staff came in and had me sign discharge papers and go over instructions on what to do when I got home. My nurse then came in and showed me the portable oxygen machine I would have to take with me wherever I went. It looked like one of those small black suitcases that roll. Oxygen would come through the filters and give me the air I needed to survive.

Finally, the time had come. It was time to leave. My hospital journey was about to be completed. So many thoughts raced in my head from the initial ride in the ambulance to my multiple days on the ventilator to the countless days of feeling hopeless and having major hallucinations. I was overwhelmed with emotion and began to cry very heavily. I could not hold in my emotions any longer. I couldn't believe I was going home to be with Tracy and Warner.

I called my wife, and she informed me she was just a few minutes away from the meeting spot behind the hospital. My nurse put another gown on me, this time from the back to the front, covering up my nakedness beneath. The other nurse gathered my items into a cart and out of the room I was wheeled. As I exited, my doctor greeted me, told me to take care, and wished me well. I thanked him for his kindness and care.

Down the elevator we went, from the top floor all the way down to the bottom level. As my nurse wheeled me out of the elevator and did a 180, I was looking out the glass windows and noticed my wife's Toyota Highlander parked next to the ambulances. She was here! Warner was here! As we got outside, the cold air and rain made me shiver, but I didn't care because I was going home!

One nurse got me next to the car while the other nurse loaded my three bags into the trunk. My nurse opened the car door and put my oxygen suitcase on the front floorboard. As I stood up, I saw the most beautiful face in the driver's seat... my Tracy! My love and my rock! I smiled and quietly got in the seat and said goodbye to my nurse.

"Call us if you need anything!" she shouted, and I gently closed the car door. I looked towards my left and was greeted with a cautious smile. I heard a voice in the backseat and looked back to see my pride and joy, my reason for living, my son Warner.

"Mom, can I hug him?"

"Of course you can," I said. "Come hug your daddy!"

He got up reluctantly and put his arms around me and we both wept a little.

"I thought I would never see you again, Daddy. I prayed for you!" During the ride home, he told me about his special prayer to God.

I took a while to get home due to the beginning of construction near our exit on Interstate 26, but we pulled into the driveway, and for the first time in a long time, I was home! But it was a different feeling of home. This was now my sanctuary, my safe place! As I entered the door with my oxygen suitcase in tow, I was greeted by my dog Zoe, who apparently didn't recognize me, maybe because of the face mask, or the fact I was in a hospital gown, or that I had lost approximately forty pounds. She barked for a few seconds, but once I said her name, the barking stopped, and she wanted her daddy!

Tracy led me to the couch and covered me up with blankets. I was in my recliner sofa seat, and it never felt so comfortable in my entire life. All three bags were dropped beside the couch. It was good to be home, but we had one more hurdle to overcome!

Within five minutes of being home, the oxygen suitcase started beeping loudly and showing a flashing red screen on the top with the words "Needs Charging. Oxygen will shut off in 2 minutes!"

What the heck? I finally made it out of the hospital and now I was going to have no oxygen and die? Tracy and Warner were frantic, and my son began to shout and scream. Tracy grabbed my packet and called the hospital nurse line and told them about the urgent issue. What I wasn't told was that the oxygen suitcase had a charger to go with it, so Tracy pulled it out of the bag as the seconds were ticking away! She plugged the charger into the wall and then into the suitcase. Then silence... was I getting oxygen? The screen went blank, then suddenly the green light came on and I could feel oxygen once again. That was too close for comfort. We calmed Warner down and every thirty minutes, he checked the cord to make sure the tank was being charged.

All three of us were sitting and Warner was obviously tired. He fell asleep in the opposite sofa recliner across the living room.

"Matthew, a lot happened to you and I have a lot of stories to tell you about the past month, some of which you probably don't remember, but do you realize you are a miracle?" Tracy asked.

I nodded my head in approval, and she began to tell me stories about my journey that I didn't know and all the people who prayed for me and how the entire community came together for her and Warner. Whether it was food (and lots of it), texts, prayer cards, or phone calls. I began to realize that there was more than what I had known. I got on Facebook and was shocked to see all the posts my friends had posted with thousands upon thousands of responses. In my heart, I felt loved! I suddenly realized that my journey had reached a lot of people, and it truly showed the...

POWER OF PRAYER!

CHAPTER 14

APRIL 19, 2021

Over a little more than three months had passed since I was released from Lexington Medical Center. Even though I returned home on January 8, 2021, my fight with bad COVID was far from over. For the first few weeks, getting up and traveling fifteen feet to the bathroom with my oxygen suitcase in tow, and then coming back, totally exhausted, as if I had just run a full Olympic marathon. I slept a lot the first month since my energy level was low. I couldn't prepare my own meal. I heavily depended on Tracy and Warner to help me through this difficult adjustment, but they both were so awesome and helped me with anything else I needed.

The next step in my journey was to see a pulmonologist. I saw Dr. Cauthen, who was actually the father of one of my son's friends at school. My first appointment was a mere five days after my hospital release. I had to do a breathing test, which I hated with a passion. They took my weight, and I was all the way down to 220 lbs. Heck, I hadn't weighed that little in almost twenty years! They took a chest x-ray and when Dr. Cauthen finally met with me. He showed me all the COVID still in my lungs. He told me it would take at least three to six months to get rid of the COVID and that I would need to be on constant oxygen. Whenever I would walk a short distance and look at my oximeter, my oxygen saturation level would be below 90%, and that was with continuous flow of oxygen. I knew I was in for the fight of my life to get back to some sense of normalcy.

With the assistance of a home health nurse and a physical therapist, who both came to my home twice a week, my journey back to normal started. In my first physical therapy session, I had to sit in a chair, then stand up with no assistance, and sit down. And I had to do it ten times. It took me almost eight minutes. We started with one lap around the large kitchen, my wife's dream kitchen, and slowly worked my way up to two and by the end of two months, I was walking for at least fifteen to twenty minutes and not getting winded at all. I was making progress. I so wanted to play golf again with Richard and Larry. I so wanted to be able to make it to Texas in July to see my goddaughter get married. I so wanted to go outside and throw the football with my son, which was our bonding time! I wanted to have a normal life, but I soon learned nothing would be normal ever again.

By the time March ended, I had my last home physical therapy session. To get up from a chair, stand, then sit back down and repeat it ten times only took me fifteen seconds! What a difference from January! I was so excited that Dr. Cauthen even challenged me to spend at least fifteen minutes at a time without oxygen but have my oximeter on to check my saturation level. At first, it was at 90%, but then a week later it crept up to 92%.

On April 10th, Tracy drove Warner and I to Lexington, so she could get Target groceries and anyone who knew my wife knew how much she loved Target. It was her and her best friend Barb's favorite thing to do in Texas- that and Kohl's! Anyway, I took off my canula and sat quietly in the back seat and was in complete shock. My oxygen saturation level was at 97%! I kept quiet until we made the entire thirty-minute trek to Lexington, and I shared the good news, to a big shout out from Warner! I kept if off the entire road home, and my oxygen didn't drop below 95%. Suddenly, there was the proverbial light at the end of the tunnel! I couldn't wait to see Dr. Cauthen in a week.

On April 19, 2021, I visited Dr. Cauthen's office. I did my breathing test, which I felt went well. My weight had increased by thirty pounds as I was finally gaining weight back from my extended hospital stay. A chest x-ray was taken, and a few minutes later, Dr. Cauthen walked into the room where Tracy and I were talking.

"Matt, look at this X-Ray," he said. "Your lungs are totally clear! You are free from COVID! The best part is you don't have to be oxygen any longer and you can resume normal activity!"

I wanted so badly to hug the life out of Dr. Cauthen,

but I just bowed my head and thanked the Lord for all the strength he had given me and gave him all the Glory. Tracy asked her usual questions and was even told I could play golf without any restrictions. As we walked out of the office with no oxygen, I felt free! I felt liberated! I felt great! But this moment was not complete without sharing with one more person.

We arrived at Warner's school at approximately 11:30am. He was in class, so Tracy went and got him. He came out quickly, and I got down on one knee and told him the good news. What happened next is a moment I will never forget. Dressed in my Chiefs Tyreek Hill jersey, I was given the biggest hug of my life from my pride and joy! I did not want to forget this moment. We hugged for about five minutes. He didn't want to let me go, and I didn't want to let him go.

When he finally backed up, he had a small tear down his right cheek, which I wiped away and told him I was back and ready to be the dad I needed to be. He smiled as big as possible and ran back to his classroom to tell his friends. What a moment and what a day! My bad COVID journey was over. Now it was time to spread the word, live life and make memories! My new lease on life started, and I wasn't going to take any moment for granted ever again. God is good because of….

THE POWER OF PRAYER!

PART THREE

CHAPTER 15

LIFE AFTER COVID

The past few years haven't been the easiest. I have had to overcome a ton of obstacles. Getting bronchitis out of nowhere at least three times a year has been one side effect. An auto-immune issue has surfaced this year. Trying to do any form of exercise and I am out of breath within twenty seconds. I get tired rather easily. I am fortunate enough to play golf, and riding in a cart certainly helps my stamina.

A month after my clearance, I got the chance to play golf with my two best buddies, Richard and Larry. Richard knows all too well about near-death experiences as he battled pancreatic cancer ten years ago. Larry, at the same time I was battling COVID, was having open heart triple bypass surgery. Needless to say, we were all glad to gather in Florence for a weekend full of golf and fellowship.

Now, Larry struggles to break 100, and I even struggle to break 120, while Richard consistently shoots or breaks 80. When playing with Richard, money is always on the line, so he decided to give us two strokes per every six holes and Larry and I played best ball. Larry and I played the best two rounds of our lives. Through the first six holes at Governor's Run, Richard was one under par and we still smoked him. Larry was bombing drives; I was hunting down flagsticks with my irons and we made almost every clutch putt. We haven't played that well since, but what a weekend to remember!

One thing that has helped me is my brothers in my fantasy football league. We meet every August in Myrtle Beach to play golf, eat a lot of food, goof off, participate in our annual fantasy draft and just have fun together.

While in the hospital and after my discharge, I heard from everyone in our group and that meant the world to me. Richard, Larry, Sean, Patrick, Mike, Tom, Ley, Chris, Grant and Joe, I want to thank you all for your encouragement during a very dark time in my life. I appreciate all the texts I got during the Buckeyes run to the National Championship Game against Alabama. I appreciate all the texts, calls and well wishes I got from you all. You are my brothers, and I love you guys. I look forward to every football season where we have our Sunday and Monday night chats filled with excitement or frustration, depending on who wins and losses.

Another thing has been the presence of my inner circle. For so many years, I was consumed with trying to have thousands upon thousands of Facebook friends. Now, my life isn't about quantity... it's about quality! My quality of life, whether the friends I keep, the precious moments I have with Warner and Tracy, or just a simple phone call to tell one of my close friends that I love them. These are the moments I truly cherish each and every day.

I have talked a lot about my faith and how important it is to me. My book is titled *My Son Saved Me*, which is actually two-fold. Yes, my son, Warner, said that special prayer, starting the prayers around the world for a miracle. What has not yet been mentioned is that God sent his only son, Jesus, to be born on this earth, live a life without sin, and to die on the cross to save us from our sins. I can truly say and believe with my whole heart that God's son was sent to save us all! All we have to do is surrender our lives to him, so that we may have everlasting life. If you don't believe me, just read one passage of the Bible, John 3:16, which reads, "God so loved the world that He gave His one and only Son, that whoever believes in Him shall not perish but have eternal life."

This powerful verse says it all! What a gift from God!

I have learned and discovered many things since I came home from the hospital in January 2021. If I leave you with anything regarding my journey, it is this... WE NEED LOVE NOW MORE THAN EVER! We need to respect others with our whole heart. Jesus teaches us to love as we are all God's children! And by all, I mean ALL! I am trying to reach out to those who see Christianity as "you must fit in this square peg" to be a Christian…. NO! All of us are different. Whether by gender, race, sexual orientation, political differences, or religion, we are all different.

If you are white, you are loved by God!
If you are black, you are loved by God!
If you are from other descents, you are loved by God!
If you are straight, you are loved by God!
If you are LGBTQIA+, you are loved by God!
If you are Republican, you are loved by God!
If you are Democrat, you are loved by God!
If you believe in God, you are loved by God!
If you don't believe in God, you are loved by God!

Nowhere in 1 Corinthians Chapter 1 does it say otherwise. We are all loved by God and are all truly worthy of God's love, even if we feel we don't deserve His grace. I often fall short of the grace given by God, but in spite of my sin, he loves me! I truly believe this and will take it with me to the grave. I believe in Heaven, and I know I will be with my mom again, laughing and playing euchre with my granddad.

I must admit, a good two years after my release from Lexington Medical Center, I struggled with survivor's guilt. Why was I saved when I was prayed for? Why did others who were prayed over die anyway? Over 1.4 million Americans and over 7 million worldwide have passed due to this dreaded COVID virus. I know personally know several people who have died when their friends and family prayed for them, so why weren't they saved? AAHH, THE $64

MILLION DOLLAR QUESTION! Let me give you my belief about life, prayer and death.

God hears our prayers. He hears them all, but something we must all learn is that we are not in control... God is! He has a plan for me, a plan for Warner, a plan for Tracy, a plan for us all. I am a firm believer that God is trying to reach us all. He uses different methods to get us to come to Him. For me, what worked was presenting in my life certain individuals to bring me to follow his son, Jesus, worked. He prepared me for my future so that I could meet my soulmate and have a life worth living.

The part I struggle with is children dying, whether it be from cancer or other dreaded diseases. Why must he take them? I am a firm believer that everyone on this earth is here for a purpose, a purpose bigger than we can even fathom or understand. When our purpose is fulfilled, he takes us to be with him. God uses people in our lives to help inspire others.

I often think back to the late Jim Valvano, legendary men's basketball coach at N.C. State. He and his "cardiac pack" miraculously won the 1983 Men's Basketball championship in one of the most thrilling finishes in Final Four history. Whittenburg's shot was short, but Charles caught it and dunked it as time expired... WHAT AN ENDNG! The dominant Houston team, known as "Phi Slamma Jamma" has been miraculously beaten. This game has gone down in history as one of the biggest championship game miracles ever.

Ten years later, ESPN hosted the first ESPYs, sort of sports version of the Oscars or Emmys. At that time,

Coach Valvano was batting cancer. He was fighting for his life and was so close to death. Yet, he was being honored with the Arthur Ashe Courage award. In the most impactful eleven-minute speech ever given, Coach Valvano stated his purpose… he was starting the Jimmy V Foundation for Cancer Research. In 1993, millions upon millions were being given to AIDS research, but hardly any towards cancer research. His famous speech wrapped up with his motto that holds true for even me today, "Don't give up, don't ever give up!"

No more than a month later, Coach Valvano died. However, more than thirty years later, his legacy lives on, as hundreds of millions of dollars have been donated to further cancer research. If not for Jimmy V, my wife's treatment she got in 2013 would not have been possible. His true passion for people and helping others, even though he knew he was going to die, inspired future generations to fight the fight!

So why am I here? What is my purpose? For me, it's simple. I want to help our struggling youth to surrender their lives to Jesus. Let him be in control and enjoy the ride. Most of all, I want all of us to spread love, not hate! We are born with love in our hearts, but we are taught to hate! I urge everyone reading this to spread love and respect for our fellow human beings. We may not agree with what they say or what lifestyle they choose, but out of the goodness of our hearts, respect them as we are all human beings. We all have hearts, and at times, all of our hearts hurt. Do you want to see a world filled with acceptance, love and respect, or a world with hate, division and war? This choice is not up to just the leaders of the world, it is up to us as individuals to live out God's word in loving our fellow humans. I can't make it any simpler than that.

Yes, there are going to be those who still hate, but we can't control them. We can only control our own thoughts, behaviors, and emotions. If you do your job and make the world a better place by doing what you can, you have fulfilled God's word.

I have no clue when my last breath will be taken on this earth. iI could be weeks, months, or many years. One thing I have learned is the power of the human spirit. We are capable of things greater than we can even imagine. Go make a difference in society, give your time and efforts to causes you believe in. If you don't leave with anything else, remember about the wondrous things were being given through…

THE POWER OF PRAYER!

ACKNOWLEDGMENTS

I have so many people to thank who have been there for me during this difficult yet rewarding journey. If I missed someone, I am sorry.

First, all glory goes to God, who is my personal Lord and Savior. With God, all things are possible.

Thank you to the staff at Lexington Medical Center who helped in their own special way to care for me and heal me of COVID.

Thank you to Northside Christian Academy and especially Pastor Crede and Ms. Brewer for your constant support of my son during a very difficult time for an eleven-year-old.

Thank you to all my cousins, especially my Cleveland cousins, for your constant texts, calls and cards. I love you all!

Thank you to my Coker family for your thoughts and prayers. Coker made me into who I am today. To my former Commissioners, whom I advised for five years, I love you guys and will always cherish the friendships we formed as I saw you grow from students to successful alumni.

Thank you to my four godchildren (Gillian, Logan, Abby and Maggie) who have given me a little bit of my youth back as I watch you all grow into wonderful adults. You were a major reason I fought so hard, and I love you all so much.

Thank you to my brother Ronnie, who is the best big brother in the entire world. I couldn't have asked for a better brother. I draw strength from you, as you have been through your own adversity, but always come out the other end golden. I love you, brother

Thank you to my special friend Pamela, who inspired me to write this book…it only took about four years, but I am now an author, and all the thanks goes to you. I love you, my friend.

Special thanks to my mother-in-law, Janet. I know I can be a pain to live with, but I truly honor, respect and love you. You were there for me when I lost my mom, and I truly value you. Love you, Mia!

Thank you to my wife, my rock, and my soulmate Tracy. God handed you to me, and I promise to take care of you and treat you better every day. You inspire me to be a better person, a better husband and a better father. I love you, sweetheart!

And to my reason for living, my son, Warner. What can I say about you? You are a wonderful human being who feels called to the ministry. Whatever you do in life, just know your dad is proud of you and loves you with all his heart. We are so much alike, and you sometimes drive me crazy, but I can't imagine life on this earth without you. Whatever you do, live your life for you! I thank God every day that he chose me to be your dad, all because of the…

POWER OF PRAYER!

Made in the USA
Columbia, SC
20 October 2024